Lützen & Bautzen 1813

The turning point

Campaign • 87

Lützen & Bautzen 1813

The turning point

Peter Hofschröer · Illustrated by Christa Hook

Series editor Lee Johnson · *Consultant editor* David G Chandler

First published in Great Britain in 2001 by Osprey Publishing,
Midland House, West Way, Botley, Oxford OX2 0PH, UK
443 Park Avenue South, New York, NY 10016, USA
Email: info@ospreypublishing.com

CIP Data for this publication is available from the British Library

ISBN-13: 978-1-85532-994-2

Typeset in Helvetica Neue and ITC New Baskerville

Editor: Lee Johnson
Design: The Black Spot
Colour bird's-eye view illustrations by The Black Spot
Cartography by The Map Studio
Battlescene artwork by Christa Hook
Indexer: Alan Rutter
Origination by PPS Grasmere Ltd., Leeds, UK
Printed in China through World Print Ltd.

07 08 09 10 11 13 12 11 10 9 8 7 6 5 4

FOR A CATALOGUE OF ALL BOOKS PUBLISHED BY
OSPREY MILITARY AND AVIATION PLEASE CONTACT:

NORTH AMERICA
Osprey Direct, C/o Random House Distribution Center,
400 Hahn Road, Westminster, MD 21157, USA
E-mail: info@ospreydirect.com

ALL OTHER REGIONS
Osprey Direct UK, P.O. Box 140, Wellingborough,
Northants, NN8 2FA, UK
E-mail: info@ospreydirect.co.uk

www.ospreypublishing.com

Acknowledgements

My thanks go to Tom Holmberg, Dominic Goh, Ed Wimble,
Todd Fisher, George Nafziger and John Cook for their
assistance in the preparation of this book.

Artist's Note

Readers may care to note that the original paintings from
which the colour plates in this book were prepared are
available for private sale. All reproduction copyright
whatsoever is retained by the Publisher. All enquiries
should be addressed to :

Scorpio Gallery, PO Box 475, Hailsham,
E. Sussex BN27 2SL UK

The publishers regret that they can enter into no
correspondence on this matter.

KEY TO MILITARY SYMBOLS

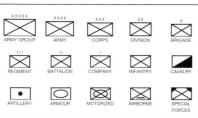

CONTENTS

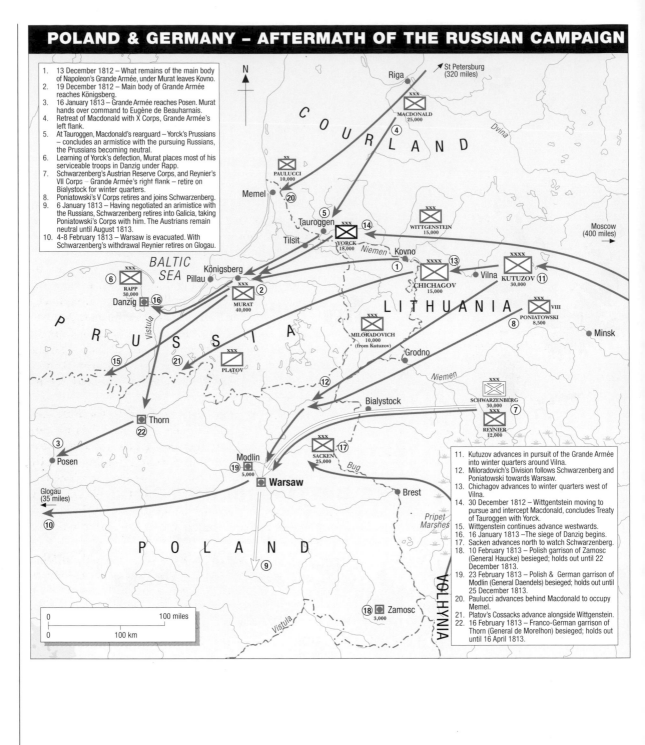

POLAND & GERMANY – AFTERMATH OF THE RUSSIAN CAMPAIGN

1. 13 December 1812 – What remains of the main body of Napoleon's Grande Armée, under Murat leaves Kovno.
2. 19 December 1812 – Main body of Grande Armée reaches Königsberg.
3. 16 January 1813 – Grande Armée reaches Posen. Murat hands over command to Eugène de Beauharnais.
4. Retreat of Macdonald with X Corps, Grande Armée's left flank.
5. At Tauroggen, Macdonald's rearguard – Yorck's Prussians – concludes an armistice with the pursuing Russians, the Prussians becoming neutral.
6. Learning of Yorck's defection, Murat places most of his serviceable troops in Danzig under Rapp.
7. Schwarzenberg's Austrian Reserve Corps, and Reynier's VII Corps – Grande Armée's right flank – retire on Bialystock for winter quarters.
8. Poniatowski's V Corps retires and joins Schwarzenberg.
9. 6 January 1813 – Having negotiated an arimistice with the Russians, Schwarzenberg retires into Galicia, taking Poniatowski's Corps with him. The Austrians remain neutral until August 1813.
10. 4-8 February 1813 – Warsaw is evacuated. With Schwarzenberg's withdrawal Reynier retires on Glogau.

11. Kutuzov advances in pursuit of the Grande Armée into winter quarters around Vilna.
12. Miloradovich's Division follows Schwarzenberg and Poniatowski towards Warsaw.
13. Chichagov advances to winter quarters west of Vilna.
14. 30 December 1812 – Wittgentstein moving to pursue and intercept Macdonald, concludes Treaty of Tauroggen with Yorck.
15. Wittgenstein continues advance westwards.
16. 16 January 1813 – The siege of Danzig begins.
17. Sacken advances north to watch Schwarzenberg.
18. 10 February 1813 – Polish garrison of Zamosc (General Haucke) besieged; holds out until 22 December 1813.
19. 23 February 1813 – Polish & German garrison of Modlin (General Daendels) besieged; holds out until 25 December 1813.
20. Paulucci advances behind Macdonald to occupy Memel.
21. Platov's Cossacks advance alongside Wittgenstein.
22. 16 February 1813 – Franco-German garrison of Thorn (General de Morelhon) besieged; holds out until 16 April 1813.

N

St Petersburg
(320 miles)

Riga

COURLAND

Dvina

MACDONALD
25,000
④

Moscow
(400 miles)

PAULUCCI
10,000

Memel
⑳

⑤

Tauroggen

WITTGENSTEIN
15,000

⑭

Tilsit

YORCK
18,000

Niemen

Kovno

①

CHICHAGOV
15,000

⑬

Vilna

KUTUZOV
30,000

⑪

BALTIC
SEA

Königsberg

Pillau

RAPP
30,000

⑥

②

MURAT
40,000

LITHUANIA

PONIATOWSKI
8,500

VIII

⑧

Minsk

Danzig ⑯

PRUSSIA

Vistula

MILORADOVICH
10,000
(from Kutuzov)

Grodno

⑮

⑳①

PLATOV

Niemen

⑫

Bialystock

SCHWARZENBERG
30,000

⑦

REYNIER
12,000

Thorn

㉒

③

Posen

Modlin

⑲
5,000

SACKEN
25,000

⑰

Bug

Brest

Warsaw

Pripet
Marshes

Glogau
(35 miles)

⑩

POLAND

⑨

VOLHYNIA

⑱ Zamosc
3,000

Vistula

0   100 miles
0   100 km

INTRODUCTION

Napoleon in 1813. Leaving his army to face its fate at the end of 1812, Napoleon returned to France to set about rebuilding his shattered forces to attempt to maintain his hold of Central Europe. He displayed considerable energy and organisational skills. (Painting by Amable-Louis-Claude Pagnest)

By the spring of 1813, Europe had been at war more or less continuously for two decades. The original cause of this instability had been the French Revolution, which had started in 1789. A certain French artillery officer of Corsican origins, one Napoleone Buonaparte, as he was then known, used the opportunity presented to gain power in France. He eventually crowned himself Emperor in 1804. Not satisfied with ruling one country, Emperor Napoleon engaged in wars of aggression, conquering and subjugating Italy, Austria and Germany. In Germany, these wars caused the collapse of the First Reich, otherwise known as the Holy Roman Empire of the German Nation. Much of Europe became his sphere of influence. Dominating Central Europe, Napoleon then came to an agreement with Russia, leaving Britain the only country still defying him in Europe. However, Britain was, thanks to her naval superiority, safe from invasion. This was due in part to Nelson's victory at Trafalgar in 1805.

Unable to gain control of the seas, Napoleon tried to force Britain into line by adopting the so-called 'Continental System'. This was an attempt at blockade in reverse. Napoleon decreed that the nations of the Continent of Europe should not trade with Britain, hoping thereby to damage Britain's economy severely. Instead, Europe's traders felt themselves put at a disadvantage. The Russians, due to their relatively underdeveloped economy, suffered the most, and they soon breached the Continental System. The invasion of 1812 was in part an attempt to bring Czar Alexander back into line.

Napoleon was essentially a dictator who owed his power to popular consent. The populace of France was happy to give its consent as long as Napoleon brought France fame, victories and above all plunder. To avoid unpopularity at home, Napoleon always tried to place as much as possible of the burden of his military conquests on the shoulders of the other nations of Europe. His armies pillaged wherever they went, constantly sending back riches and trophies of war to Paris. Germany in particular suffered severely from this plundering. Prussia had to pay a massive indemnity to France after the catastrophic defeats of 1806, which greatly impoverished the country. Without the resources of Central Europe to fuel his military machine, Napoleon would have been forced to draw more heavily on those of France. Napoleon needed the resources of Central Europe to sustain his dictatorship. His domination of Germany was of vital importance to the continuation of his dynasty.

As far as the other powers of continental Europe were concerned, the fate of Germany would determine the fate of Europe. The Czar of Russia wanted to extent his sphere of influence ever further westwards. The Emperor of Austria wanted to see the German States re-formed into the old First Reich, under Austrian domination. Meanwhile, Czar Alexander groomed King Frederick William III of Prussia to act as his protégé in Germany. The Austrian Emperor Francis I, while wanting to see Napoleon thrown out of Germany, did not want to see Alexander step into his boots. Initially, Francis, acting on advice from the great statesman Metternich, hesitated. He awaited events before committing himself, only doing so in the autumn of 1813. Russia's Great Patriotic War of 1812 became Germany's War of Liberation of 1813. This led to Napoleon's First Abdication of 1814 and the collapse of his Empire.

Background to the Campaign

The army that Napoleon assembled for the 1812 Campaign was at the time the largest ever assembled in history. It marched into Russia in 1812, but only a shattered remnant returned. Napoleon, until then at the peak of his power, rushed back to Paris to deal with a possible uprising against his regime. He left one of his lieutenants, Eugène de Beauharnais, to safeguard his interests in Germany. Meanwhile, Napoleon stabilised his position at home and then began to rebuild his depleted military forces. The Russians too needed time to repair and rebuild their exhausted army before daring to advance into Central Europe. The consequences of the French disaster on the situation in Germany were now becoming apparent. The King of Prussia, Frederick William III, procrastinated, believing the time not yet ripe to make a stand against the oppressor of his kingdom. The first to strike a blow against the 'Corsican tyrant' was the Prussian General Yorck. He was the commander of the Prussian Auxiliary Corps, a body of some 20,000 men Prussia had been obliged to contribute to Napoleon's 1812 expedition. During the French retreat Yorck had managed to detach himself from the rest of the Grande Armée and then commenced negotiations with Diebitsch, the commander of the Russian forces in the area. They agreed to the Convention of Tauroggen on 30 December 1812 which 'neutralised' this Prussian contingent. Yorck's Corps then occupied East Prussia in collaboration with the Czar's forces. Here, it formed the core of an anti-Napoleonic rebellion. While Prussia officially adopted a course of hesitant neutrality, one of its provinces had de facto declared war against the French. Her king now only needed assurances of Russian support from Czar Alexander before he too threw in his lot with the Russians. Having gained these assurances at a meeting with the Czar in the Prussian province of Silesia in February 1813, Prussia officially declared war on France in March of that year. The stage was now set for the Spring Campaign of 1813.

Many historians regard the winter of 1812 as marking the turning point in Napoleon's domination of the Continent of Europe. The demise of his Grande Armée of 600,000 men in the dust and snow of Russia meant that he would never again be able to attempt to dominate that country. However, until he suffered a decisive military defeat in Central Europe, Napoleon remained a power to be reckoned with. The rapidity with which he replaced his lost forces during the winter of 1812–13 demonstrated this amply. While the rest of Europe hesitated to challenge the wobbling throne of the Emperor of France, Napoleon set about filling the vacuum that appeared in the aftermath of the Russian disaster. He marched into Germany early in 1813 at the head of a new army, determined to re-establish his hegemony in Central Europe. It

Alexander I, Czar of Russia. Once Napoleon had been driven out of Russia, the Czar's forces moved into Central Europe. Alexander saw himself as a liberator. (Lithograph by Katzler)

appeared only the brave or foolhardy risked standing against him. Napoleon was confronted by a force of Russian and Prussian troops inferior in numbers to his own. They were however determined to bring Napoleon to battle and defeat him. In the spring of 1813 they were to come within a hair's breadth of achieving this aim. Both major battles were bloody and bitter affairs, and although Napoleon won tactical victories, driving back his adversaries on both occasions, the spring campaign of 1813 marked the strategic turning point in Napoleonic Europe. If Napoleon could not defeat the Russians and Prussians with his superior numbers, then Europe had, at last, the chance of bringing the 'tyrant' to bay. This would require the formation of another great coalition of France's enemies, but Russia and Prussia had cracked Napoleon's mask of invincibility. From the spring of 1813 the tide began to run ever more strongly against Bonaparte – he had lost his last real chance of preserving his dynasty.

CHRONOLOGY

The War of 1812
24 June 1812 Napoleon invades Russia.
7 September 1812 The Battle of Borodino.
18 October 1812 Napoleon withdraws from Moscow.
28 November 1812 The crossing of the Berezina.
30 December 1812 The Convention of Tauroggen is signed. Yorck's Prussian Auxiliary Corps defects.

The War of Liberation 1813 – The Spring Campaign
January 1813 The East Prussian Estates rise up against Napoleon.
3 February 1813 The King of Prussia issues an edict calling all men to arms.
27 February 1813 Treaty of Kalisch. The Prussians join the Russians against Napoleon.
4 March 1813 The French withdraw from Berlin.
12 March 1813 The French abandon Hamburg.
17 March 1813 Prussia declares war on France. The Prussian Landwehr is founded.
5 April 1813 Battle of Möckern.
25 April 1813 Napoleon arrives in Erfurt.
28 April 1813 Wittgenstein replaces Kutusov as commander of the Russian Army.
2 May 1813 Battle of Lützen (Grossgörschen).
12 May 1813 The Saxon General von Thielemann, commander of the fortress of Torgau, crosses over to the Allies.
20-21 May 1813 Battle of Bautzen.
26 May 1813 Combat at Hainau.
26 May 1813 Barclay de Tolly Replaces Wittgenstein as commander-in-chief of the Russian army.
4 June 1813 Armistice of Pläswitz. End of the Spring Campaign.

OPPOSING COMMANDERS

FRENCH COMMANDERS

Napoleon Bonaparte (1769-1821), Emperor of France. Napoleon Bonaparte was undoubtedly one of the great military captains of history. He had held Europe in thrall for over a decade, plunging the Continent into its most destructive wars for centuries. Napoleon was essentially a dictator and did little to encourage initiative among his subordinates lest a rival should emerge. His style of command was centralised, and the plan of campaign was a matter Napoleon kept to himself. His staff's role was not advisory; it was functionary, being there merely to execute its master's orders. Such a system worked well in the early days of Bonaparte's campaigning in the Revolutionary Wars. However, this structure was cumbersome when attempting to control armies of the size used in the latter part of the Napoleonic Wars. The lack of initiative on the part of his subordinates could cause difficulties, as when Ney was caught out by the Allied movements on the morning of 2 May 1813. Three weeks later at Bautzen, Ney failed to properly execute the flanking movement ordered by Napoleon. It took Napoleon's personal intervention to bring matters under control again. The larger armies of the later wars required officers capable of independent command who fully grasped the Emperor's plans. However, Napoleon always had an eye on Paris and needed to be seen as the sole victor of his battles. He could not allow his subordinates to play too big a role in achieving the victories, lest they steal his glory. This inherent conflict of interests eventually played a role in Napoleon's downfall.

Having expended so much horseflesh in Russia, Napoleon was particularly weak in cavalry, which had a noticeable effect on his handling of the campaign. The cavalry were his eyes and ears, and facing a greatly superior number of allied cavalry, Napoleon was essentially deaf and blind for much of the time. Lacking detailed knowledge of Allied positions, movements and intentions, he was at a great disadvantage that was only in part compensated for by his superiority in numbers.

Napoleon did as well as he could in the circumstances. He no longer had the army that had triumphed at Austerlitz and Auerstadt, nor was he facing his enemies of 1805-06. Instead of leading veterans against ponderous and easily demoralised opponents, Napoleon faced a gruelling slogging match against hardy Russians and determined Prussians. Nevertheless, his dynamism and tactical flair remained, as his lightning reaction to events at Lützen showed, while his plan for the Battle of Bautzen on 20/21 May 1813 was ahead of its time. But by 1813, Napoleon had simply run out of luck. He was also running out of time.

Frederick William III, King of Prussia. Often regarded as a weak king, Frederick William showed considerable courage when he threw in his lot with Alexander. His gamble paid off, with Napoleon being finally driven from Germany after the Battle of Leipzig in October 1813. (Copy of a painting by François Gérard dated 1814)

Michel Ney (1769-1815), Marshal of France. Ney was one of the more colourful characters of this period. Noted for his bravery, he was much respected by his men. Ney had also shown himself a highly capable corps commander, working his way up the ranks after having joined a regiment of hussars in 1787. Ney was also to play a significant role in the Spring Campaign of 1813. He failed to properly secure the positions of his corps during the night of 1–2 May, allowing the Allies to launch the surprise attack that began the Battle of Lützen. Had the Allies not handled their advance to contact so badly, they may well have won a decisive victory over Napoleon. Ney again had the fate of France in his hands during his flanking march at the battle of Bautzen. At a crucial stage, he delayed his advance, awaiting orders from Napoleon, then failed to use his initiative and break into the rear of the Allies, which would have decided the battle and campaign. Ney is often the scapegoat of Napoleon's apologists. As we shall see, Napoleon was aware that Ney had not sent patrols out to screen his camp at Grossgörschen. Furthermore, it was understandable for Ney to enquire of Napoleon as to his next move at Bautzen once he had heard the sounds of gunfire. The Emperor had not shared the details of his plan of action for Bautzen with Ney. As such it was difficult for Ney to assess the best course of action.

ALLIED COMMANDERS

Ludwig Adolph Peter, Prince of Sayn and Wittgenstein (1769-1843). As a boy, Wittgenstein joined the Page Corps of the Semenov Regiment with the rank of sergeant. In 1789, he was transferred to the Horse Guard Regiment, being promoted to lieutenant the next year. He received his baptism of fire in the Polish Campaign of 1795. He rose quickly through the ranks, becoming a full colonel in 1798 and major-general a year later. Made colonel-in-chief of the Mariupol Hussar Regiment in 1801, he distinguished himself at Austerlitz in 1805. He fought the Turks in 1806 before fighting the French at Friedland in 1807. He defended St Petersburg in 1812, taking command of the Prusso-Russian army in 1813, commanding it at Lützen and Bautzen. Due to his rather lack-lustre performance, Wittgenstein was replaced by Barclay de Tolly on 26 May 1813.

Mikhail Barclay de Tolly, (1761-1818). Barclay was the one Russian general capable of rising to the challenge of command in Germany in 1813. His military experience had started in 1788 in fighting against the Turks. He fought the Swedes in 1790 and saw action in Poland from 1792 to 1794. In 1806, he commanded the vanguard of Bennigsen's army, winning a battle at Pultusk and being wounded at Eylau. He distinguished himself in Finland in 1808 and 1809, becoming Minister of War in 1810. In 1812, although he favoured withdrawing in the face of Napoleon's advance into Russia, public opinion forced him to offer battle at Smolensk, the 'gateway to Old Russia'. A German-speaker, he was not popular in Russia and was removed from command for his views on the best strategy to adopt against Napoleon's invasion. The Russian Kutusov, considered a better man to defend the soil of Mother Russia, replaced him, eventually leading the army into Germany in 1813. Wittgenstein took over the command of the army on Kutusov's death, but did not distinguish himself. On 26 May 1813, Barclay was given command of the Russian forces in Germany. He was known for his caution and pedantry, but the Spring Campaign ended before he was able to influence its events in an appreciable way.

Gebhardt Leberecht von Blücher (1742-1819). Blücher's military career began at the tender age of fourteen in the Swedish cavalry. This was normal as Sweden held territories on the Baltic coast of Germany at this time and her army drilled according to Frederician regulations with orders given in the German language. The Prussians took him prisoner in 1760 during the Seven Years War, and he joined Belling's regiment of hussars, later gaining a reputation for wild behaviour off the battlefield and aggression on it. Throughout this period, he was firmly in favour of dealing with French encroachments into Germany by firm military action and his successes in the Revolutionary Wars added to his reputation. At the Battle of Auerstadt in 1806, he mishandled the Prussian cavalry, attacking Davout's men too early, but made up for this fighting a spirited retreat to Lübeck on the Baltic coast. He added his stature to the reform movement in the Prussian army that Scharnhorst and Gneisenau greatly influenced. A passionate man, his despair at Prussia's humiliation following the defeats in 1806 caused a nervous breakdown. He gleefully took up his sabre again at the beginning of 1813. By now, the Prussian army had adopted a system of dual command for its larger formations. Blücher commanded a corps in the Spring Campaign with first Scharnhorst and then Gneisenau being his chief-of-staff. The individual genius of Napoleon was countered with the collective genius of the Prussian General Staff. At Bautzen, for example, Gneisenau tempered Blücher's natural aggression, persuading him to withdraw once Ney's flanking move became effective.

The Russian General Diebitsch and the Prussian General Yorck first met on the evening of 25 December 1812. Their negotiations took the Prussian contingent out of the Grande Armée and precipitated Prussia's uprising against Napoleon. (Drawing by Richard Knötel)

THE OPPOSING ARMIES

Hans David Ludwig Yorck, later Graf von Wartenburg. (Print after von Gebauer)

THE FRENCH ARMY

Napoleon marched into Russia in 1812 with over 600,000 men. Of this force, no less than 500,000 perished, along with around 150,000 horses. Besides that, he lost around 1,000 cannon and 25,000 vehicles. With substantial forces committed to the Peninsular Campaign and with part of his veterans tied down in garrisons in fortresses in Central Europe, Napoleon had to raise an entirely new army around a backbone of about 100,000 men. These men came from several sources.

A cadre of 20,000 men consisted of officers, NCOs, dismounted cavalry troopers, etc., who returned from Russia. In addition 2,000 men came from 20 artillery companies that had until then been on garrison duty in Prussia. The depots provided an additional 10,000 men fit for service. Around 7,000 were seconded from 98 ships' companies and four naval artillery regiments provided a further 12,000 veterans and 4,000 recruits. France's police forces supplied around 1,000 municipal guards from Paris, 4,000 men from the Departmental Reserve Companies and 3,000 mounted gendarmes, the latter largely former cavalry officers and NCOs. Finally 40,000 veterans were drawn from the forces in Spain.

In addition to this backbone of around 100,000, Napoleon raised new formations. The 1st Contingent of the National Guard provided 78,000 men. These had been called up in 1812 to conduct internal security duties in France and were fully clothed and equipped. In spring 1813, they had the best part of a year's paramilitary service behind them. From this force, 22 infantry regiments were formed along with three artillery regiments. In addition the Class of 1813 had been called up in September 1812. These 137,000 men had just started training at the beginning of 1813.

Napoleon had, on paper at least, 315,000 men at his immediate disposal from France alone. This was a significant force. In March and April 1813, those men available to the field army were organised as follows:

Formation	Commander	Strength
I Corps	Davoût	20,000 men, 16 guns
II Corps	Victor	12,000 men, 16 guns
III Corps	Ney	46,000 men, 74 guns
IV Corps	Bertrand	18,000 men, 42 guns
V Corps	Lauriston	16,000 men, 51 guns
VI Corps	Marmont	24,000 men, 62 guns
VII Corps	Reynier	4,000 men, 4 guns
XI Corps	Macdonald	22,000 men, 53 guns
XII Corps	Oudinot	24,000 men, 40 guns
I Cavalry Corps	Latour-Maubourg	3,500 men
II Cavalry Corps	Sébastiani	4,000 men
Total	**Field Army**	**193,500 men, 358 guns**

New formations arriving from France and Germany constantly reinforced this army. Including fortress garrisons, Napoleon had, by the start of hostilities, an army of around 380,000 men in Germany. Impressive as these figures may seem Napoleon's army was particularly lacking in cavalry. Of the above figure little more than 27,000 were mounted troops. This was a disproportionately small figure for any Napoleonic army, particularly when faced by the mounted formations available to the Russians and Prussians at this time. This lack of cavalry in 1813 was to play a significant role in Napoleon's defeat.

The French Imperial Guard was an élite force including infantry, cavalry and artillery formations. The infantry was divided into the Old and the Young Guard. The Old Guard was formed from the most senior veterans and the Young Guard from the pick of the new recruits. The Guard Cavalry consisted of both heavy and light regiments. The light regiments included chasseurs à cheval and lancers. The heavy cavalry consisted of the gendarmes d'élite, grenadiers à cheval, and dragoons. The Guard also had its own artillery batteries.

Other than the Imperial Guard, there were two types of infantry in the French army, the line regiments and the light regiments. It is unlikely that the difference between the two was much more than a name and a uniform, although it is possible that the light infantry contained a better calibre of recruit. Each regiment theoretically consisted of four battalions, but in the conditions of spring 1813, this number varied, with some regiments consisting of a single battalion others of several. Armament was theoretically the Charleville musket, but after so many years at war and particularly after the great losses of matériel in 1812, it is quite probable that several patterns were carried. The contingents for the Confederation of the Rhine often used locally manufactured weapons or captured supplies.

The line cavalry was also divided into heavy and light regiments. The heavy cavalry consisted of armoured cuirassiers and dragoons. Their main role was to ride down wavering and broken enemy infantry on the battlefield, although it was normal for the heavy cavalry to perform other functions, including those traditionally the role of the light cavalry. The light cavalry consisted of hussars, chasseurs à cheval and lancers. The hussars and chasseurs were mounted on nimble, faster horses and were often employed in scouting and pursuit roles off the battlefield and in the skirmish role on it. The lancers were essentially light cavalrymen, but their armament leant itself to a role as battle cavalry.

The French army used two main calibres of artillery, the 8-pdr and the 12-pdr. A field battery normally consisted of six of these pieces plus two howitzers. The horse artillery used either 6- or 8-pdrs. Their gunners were mounted to facilitate rapid movement.

France's Allies

At the beginning of 1813, both Austria and Prussia were theoretically still allies of France. The Austrian contingent to the Grande Armée of 1812 retired into the fortress town of Cracow for 'safety' from the Russians. From then until August 1813, the Austrians then adopted a policy of 'wait-and-see'. As the Prussian contingent had already declared its 'neutrality' at Tauroggen on 30 December 1812, it would be unrealistic to expect the Franco-Prussian alliance to continue.

The Italian contingent had been decimated and scattered. It would take some time before much help would come from this quarter.

The Poles, loyal allies of Napoleon, were also in the process of re-forming their forces. As the Russians had occupied the Duchy of Warsaw, as the Polish state was known at that time, it was unlikely that many new recruits would be forthcoming.

The German allies of the states of the Confederation of the Rhine were however in a position to provide aid quickly, should they want to do so. At the beginning of 1813, a cadre of around 20,000 men and 4,500 horses were available in the depots. However, in Northern Germany there was every indication of a forthcoming anti-French uprising, so the Napoleonic puppet states of Westphalia and Berg needed to keep their armies at home for internal security. The King of Saxony had yet to commit himself either way, although his contingent to the Grande Armée of 1812 under Reynier did accept orders from Viceroy Eugène de Beauharnais in the opening phase of the campaign.

Only the Catholic south of Germany could be relied on. However, as their contingents of 1812 had been all but wiped out, it would take some time for new formations to be raised and trained. For once, Napoleon would have to depend on France providing him with much of his manpower requirements. This would do little for his regime's popularity.

ORDERS-OF-BATTLE

The following abbreviations are used throughout this order-of-battle:

Coy = Company
GD = Général-de-division
MG = Major-General
LG = Lieutenant-General
Inf. = Infantry
Prov. = Provisional
Regt. = Regiment

Glossary
Oberst = Colonel
Oberstlt. = Lieut.-Colonel

Notes:
The number in brackets after the designation of a body of troops is either the number of battalions (infantry), squadrons (cavalry) or guns (artillery) in the respective formation.

FRENCH ARMY, 2 MAY 1813

FRENCH IMPERIAL GUARD:
Marshal Mortier

OLD GUARD DIVISION:
GD Baron Roguet

1st Brigade Rottembourg
Grenadiers (1)
Chasseurs (1)
2nd Voltigeurs Regt. (1)
2nd Tirailleurs Regt. (1)

2nd Brigade
Royal Italian Guard Chasseurs (1)
Velites (2)

Cavalry
Guards of Honour (3)
Italian Guard Dragoons (1)

2 foot batteries, 1 horse battery (line artillery)
(20)

1ST DIVISION OF THE YOUNG GUARD:
GD Dumoustier

1st Brigade Berthezène
Grenadiers (1)
Chasseurs (1)
1st Battalion Fusiliers-Chasseurs
1st Battalion Fusiliers-Grenadiers

2nd Brigade Lanusse
1st Voltigeur Regt. (2)
6th Voltigeur Regt. (2)
2nd Voltigeur Regt. (1)
2nd Tirailleur Regt. (1)
1st Tirailleur Regt. (2)
6th Tirailleur Regt. (2)
7th Tirailleur Regt. (2)

Artillery
2 foot batteries (Young Guard) (8 each)
3 foot batteries (Old Guard) (8 each)
2 horse batteries (6 each)

GUARD CAVALRY:
Marshal Bessières

1st Lancers (4)
2nd Lancers (4)
Chasseurs à Cheval (4)
Dragoons (4)
Grenadiers à Cheval (4)
Gendarmes d'élite (1)
Berg Lancers (1)

III CORPS:
Marshal Ney

8TH DIVISION:
GD Count Souham

1st Brigade Chemineau
6th Prov. Light Inf. Regt. (5)
14th Prov. Line Inf. Regt. (5)

2nd Brigade Lamour
21st Prov. Line Inf. Regt. (2)
24th Prov. Line Inf. Regt. (2)
22nd Line Inf. Regt. (4)

2 foot batteries (8 each)

9TH DIVISION:
GD Count Brenier

1st Brigade Grillot
2nd Prov. Light Inf. Regt. (2)
29th. Light Inf. Regt. (2)
136th. Line Inf. Regt. (4)

2nd Brigade
138th Line Inf. Regt. (4)
145th Line Inf. Regt. (4)

2 foot batteries (8 each)

10TH DIVISION:
GD Baron Girard

1st Brigade Goris
4th. Prov. Light Inf. Regt. (2)
139th. Line Inf. Regt. (4)

2nd Brigade van Dedem
140th Line Inf. Regt. (4)
141st Line Inf. Regt. (4)

2 foot batteries (8 each)

11TH DIVISION:
GD Baron Ricard

1st Brigade Tarayre
9th Light Inf. Regt. (2)
17th Prov. Line Inf. Regt. (2)
18th Prov. Line Inf. Regt. (2)

2nd Brigade Dumoulin
142nd Line Inf. Regt. (4)
144th. Line Inf. Regt. (4)

2 foot batteries (8 each)

39TH DIVISION:
GD Count Marchand

1st Brigade von Stockhorn
1st Baden Inf. Regt. (1),
3rd Baden Inf. Regt. Grand Duke (2)

2nd Brigade Prince Emil of Hesse
1st Hessian Light Inf. Regt. (2)
Hessian Life Guard Regt. (2)
Hessian Guard Regt. (2)

3rd Brigade
Frankfurter Inf. Regt. (1)

1/2 Baden foot battery (4), 1 Hessian foot
battery (8)

CAVALRY BRIGADE:
GD Count Kellermann

Brigade Laboissière
10th Hussar Regt. (4)
1st Baden Dragoon Regt. (4)

Reserve Artillery - not yet arrived. (7 foot batteries, 2 horse batteries).

IV CORPS:
GD Count Bertrand

12TH DIVISION:
GD Count Morand

1st Brigade Bellair
3rd Prov. Light Regt. (2)
13th Line Regt. (5)

2nd Brigade Nagle
2nd Prov. Illyrian Regt. (2)
23rd Line Regt. (4)

2 foot battery (8), 1 horse battery (6)

15th (Italian) Division GD de Peyri

1st Brigade Martelli
1st (Italian) Line Regt. (2)
4th (Italian) Line Regt. (4)

2nd Brigade Santo-Andrea
6th (Italian) Line Regt. (2)

3rd Brigade Moroni
Milan Guard Battalion
7th (Italian) Line Regt. (4)

2 foot batteries (8 each)

38TH (WÜRTTEMBERG) DIVISION:
GD von Franquemont

1st Brigade von Stockmayer
9th (Württemberg) Light Regt. (1)
10th (Württemberg) Light Regt. (1)
7th (Württemberg) Line Regt. (2)

2nd Brigade von Neusser
1st (Württemberg) Line Regt. (2)
2nd (Württemberg) Line Regt. (2)

Cavalry Brigade Briche
2nd (Neapolitan) Chasseurs à Cheval (2)

1 foot battery (6), 1 horse battery (6)

VI CORPS:
Marshal Marmont

20TH DIVISION:
GD Count Compans

1st Brigade Calcault
3rd Naval Artillery Regt. (2)
1st Naval Artillery Regt. (4)
2nd Brigade Joubert
20th Prov. Line Regt. (2)
32nd Light Inf. Regt. (2)

2 foot batteries (8 each)

21ST DIVISION:
GD Count Bonnet

1st Brigade Buquet
2nd Naval Artillery Regt. (6)
4th Naval Artillery Regt. (3)

2nd Brigade Jamin
37th Light Regt. (4)
Regt. Joseph Napoleon (Spanish) (1)

2 foot batteries (8 each)

22ND DIVISION:
GD Baron Friederichs

1st Brigade Ficatier
23rd Light Regt. (2)
11th Prov. Line Inf. Regt. (2)

13th Prov. Line Inf. Regt. (2)

2nd Brigade Coehorn
16th Prov. Regt. (2)
15th Line Inf. Regt. (2)
70th Line Inf. Regt. (2)
121st Line Inf. Regt. (2)

7th Chevauleger Regt. (2)

2 foot batteries (8 each)

**(23RD DIVISION IN
THE PROCESS OF FORMING)**

Reserve Artillery

2 foot batteries (1 of 8, 1 of 6 guns)

XI CORPS
Marshal Macdonald

31ST DIVISION:
GD Fressinet

1st Brigade Labassée
10th Prov. Line Inf. Demi-Brigade (4)
11th Prov. Line Inf. Demi-Brigade (2)

2nd Brigade Schobert
12th Prov. Line Inf. Demi-Brigade (3)
13th Prov. Line Inf. Demi-Brigade (3)
Neapolitan Élite Regt. (2)
3rd Line Inf. Regt. (1)
105th Line Inf. Regt. (1)
127th Line Inf. Regt. (1)

1 foot battery (8)

35TH DIVISION:
GD Baron Gérard

1st Brigade Le Sénécal
6th Line Inf. Regt. (2)
112th Line Inf. Regt. (4)

2nd Brigade Zucchi (Italians)
2nd (Italian) Light Inf. Regt. (2)
5th (Italian) Line Inf. Regt. (4)

2 French foot batteries (8 each)
1 Italian foot battery (8)

36TH DIVISION:
GD Count Charpentier

1st Brigade Simmer
14th Light Inf. Regt. (2)
22nd Light Inf. Regt. (4)

2nd Brigade Meunier
14th Prov. Line Inf. Demi-Brigade (3)
15th Prov. Line Inf. Demi-Brigade (2)

2 foot batteries (8 each)

1ST CAVALRY CORPS:
GD Count Latour-Maubourg

1st Light Division: GD Bruyères
3rd Light Division: GD Chastel
1st Heavy Division: GD Bordessoulle
3rd Heavy Division: GD Doumerc

1 horse battery (6)

FRENCH ARMY
20–21 MAY

IV CORPS:
GD Count Bertrand

12TH DIVISION:
GD Count Morand

1st Brigade Bellair
3rd Prov. Light Regt. (2)
13th Line Regt. (5)

2nd Brigade Sicard
2nd Prov. Illyrian Regt. (2)
23rd Line Regt. (4)

2 foot battery (8), 1 horse battery (6)

15TH (ITALIAN) DIVISION:
GD de Peyri

1st Brigade Martelli
1st (Italian) Line Regt. (2)
4th (Italian) Line Regt. (4)

2nd Brigade Santo-Andrea
6th (Italian) Line Regt. (2)

3rd Brigade Moroni
Milan Guard Battalion
7th (Italian) Line Regt. (4)
Cavalry Brigade Briche
2nd Neapolitan Chasseurs à Cheval (2)

2 foot batteries (8 each)

38TH (WÜRTTEMBERG) DIVISION:
GD von Franquemont

1st Brigade von Stockmayer
9th (Württemberg) Light Regt. (1)
10th (Württemberg) Light Regt. (1)
7th (Württemberg) Line Regt. (2)

2nd Brigade von Neusser
1st (Württemberg) Line Regt. (2)
2nd (Württemberg) Line Regt. (2)

1 foot battery (6), 1 horse battery (6)

From the IV Cavalry Corps

1st Brigade Briche
19th Chasseurs à Cheval Regt. (1)
2nd Neapolitan Chasseurs à Cheval (attached
to 15th Division)

4th Brigade von Stell
1st (Württemberg) Chevauleger Regt. Prince
Adam (4)
2nd (Württemberg) Chevauleger Regt. (4)

2 horse artillery batteries (6 each)

VI CORPS:
Marshal Marmont

20TH DIVISION:
GD Count Compans

1st Brigade Calcault
3rd Naval Artillery Regt. (2)
1st Naval Artillery Regt. (4)

2nd Brigade Joubert
20th Prov. Line Regt. (2)
32nd Light Inf. Regt. (2)

2 foot batteries (8 each)

21ST DIVISION:
GD Count Bonnet

1st Brigade Buquet
2nd Naval Artillery Regt. (6)
4th Naval Artillery Regt. (3)

2nd Brigade Jamin
37th Light Regt. (4)
Regt. Joseph Napoleon (Spanish) (1)

2 foot batteries (8 each)

22ND DIVISION:
GD Baron Friederichs

1st Brigade Ficatier
23rd Light Regt. (2)
11th Prov. Line Inf. Regt. (2)
13th Prov. Line Inf. Regt. (2)

2nd Brigade Coehorn
16th Prov. Regt. (2)
15th Line Inf. Regt. (2)
70th Line Inf. Regt. (2)
121st Line Inf. Regt. (2)

7th Chevauleger Regt. (2)

2 foot batteries (8 each)

**(23RD DIVISION IN
THE PROCESS OF FORMING)**

Reserve Artillery

2 foot batteries (1 of 8, 1 of 6 guns)

XI CORPS
Marshal Macdonald

31ST DIVISION:
GD Fressinet

1st Brigade Labassée
10th Prov. Line Inf. Demi-Brigade (4)
11th Prov. Line Inf. Demi-Brigade (2)

2nd Brigade Schobert
12th Prov. Line Inf. Demi-Brigade (3)
13th Prov. Line Inf. Demi-Brigade (3)

3rd Brigade Bardet
Neapolitan Élite Regt. (2)
3rd Line Inf. Regt. (1)
105th Line Inf. Regt. (1)
127th Line Inf. Regt. (1)

1 foot battery (8)

35TH DIVISION:
GD Ledru des Essarts

1st Brigade Le Sénécal
6th Line Inf. Regt. (2)
112th Line Inf. Regt. (4)

2nd Brigade Zucchi (Italians)
2nd (Italian) Light Inf. Regt. (2)
5th (Italian) Line Inf. Regt. (4)

Cavalry
4th (Italian) Chasseur à Cheval Regt. (1)
Würzburg Chevaulegers (1)

2 French foot batteries (8 each)
1 Italian horse battery (8)

36TH DIVISION:
GD Count Charpentier

1st Brigade Simmer
14th Light Inf. Regt. (2)
22nd Light Inf. Regt. (4)

2nd Brigade Meunier
14th Prov. Line Inf. Demi-Brigade (3)
15th Prov. Line Inf. Demi-Brigade (2)

2 foot batteries (8 each)

XII CORPS:
Marshal Oudinot

13TH DIVISION:
GD Baron Pacthod

1st Brigade Pourailly
1st Light Inf. Regt. (1)
12th Prov. Line Inf. Regt. (2)
67th Line Inf. Regt. (2)
7th Line Inf. Regt. (2)

2nd Brigade Cacault
4th Neapolitan Light Regt. (3)
101st Line Regt. (3)

2 foot battery (8 each)
1 (Italian) horse battery (6)

14TH DIVISION:
GD Baron Lorencez

1st Brigade Gruyer
52nd Line Inf. Regt. (2)
137th Line Inf. Regt. (3)

Brigade Brun de Villeret
18th Light Inf. Regt. (2)
156th Line Regt. (3)
Illyrian Inf. Regt. (1)

2 foot batteries (8 each)

29TH (BAVARIAN) DIVISION:
LG von Raglowitsch

1st Brigade Beckers
1st Combined Light Battalion
1st Combined Inf. Regt. (1)

Reserve
2nd Combined Inf. Regt. (1)
13th Infantry Regt. (1)

2nd Brigade Maillot de la Treille
2nd Combined Light Battalion
1st Combined Inf. Regt. (2)
2nd Combined Inf. Regt. (2)

Cavalry: Seyssel d'Aix
Combined Regiment of Chevaulegers (6)

2 foot batteries (6 each)

1ST CAVALRY CORPS:
GD Count Latour-Maubourg

1st Light Division: GD Bruyères
3rd Light Division: GD Chastel
1st Heavy Division: GD de Bordessoulle
3rd Heavy Division: GD Doumerc

1 horse battery (6)

FRENCH IMPERIAL GUARD:
Marshal Mortier

OLD GUARD DIVISION:
GD Baron Roguet

1st Grenadiers à Pied (2)
2nd Grenadiers à Pied (1)
1st Chasseurs à Pied (2)
2nd Chasseurs à Pied (1)
Velites (2)

1 battery Foot Artillery of the Old Guard (8)

1ST DIVISION OF THE YOUNG GUARD:
GD Dumoustier

1st Brigade Mouton (?)
1st Battalion Fusiliers-Chasseurs
1st Battalion Fusiliers-Grenadiers
2nd Tirailleurs Regt. (2)

2nd Brigade Lanusse
1st Voltigeur Regt. (2)
6th Voltigeur Regt. (2)
2nd Voltigeur Regt. (2)

3rd Brigade Tindal
1st Tirailleur Regt. (2)
6th Tirailleur Regt. (2)
7th Tirailleur Regt. (2)

3 foot batteries of the Young Guard (8 each)

2ND DIVISION OF THE YOUNG GUARD:
GD Barrois

1st Brigade Rottembourg
1st Tirailleurs Regt. (2)
2nd Tirailleurs Regt. (2)

2nd Brigade Mouton-Duvernet
Flankers (1)
Fusiliers-Chasseurs (1)
Fusiliers-Grenadiers (1)

3rd Brigade Boyeldieu
3rd Tirailleurs Regt. (2)
7th Voltigeurs Regt. (2)

2 foot batteries of the Young Guard (8 each)

Artillery

2 foot batteries (Young Guard) (8 each)
3 foot batteries (Old Guard) (8 each)
2 horse batteries (6 each)

GUARD CAVALRY

1ST DIVISION:
GD Lefebvre-Desnoëttes

Berg Lancers (1)
1st Lancers (4)

2nd Lancers (4)

2ND DIVISION:
GD d'Ornano

Chasseurs à Cheval (4)
Dragoons (4)
Grenadiers à Cheval (4)
Gendarmes d'élite (1)

Artillery

5 foot batteries, 4 horse batteries (8 each)

III CORPS:
Marshal Ney

16TH DIVISION:
GD Maison

1st Brigade Avril
151st Line Regt. (4)

2nd Brigade (Not present)

3rd Brigade Penne
153rd Line Regt. (3)

2 foot batteries (8 each)

8TH DIVISION:
GD Count Souham

1st Brigade Chasseraux
6th Prov. Light Inf. Regt. (2)
10th Prov. Light Inf. Regt. (2)
14th Prov. Line Inf. Regt. (2)
19th Prov. Line Inf. Regt. (2)

2nd Brigade Lamour
21st Prov. Line Inf. Regt. (2)
24th Prov. Line Inf. Regt. (2)
22nd Line Inf. Regt. (4)

2 foot batteries (8 each)

9TH DIVISION:
GD Delmas

1st Brigade Anthing
2nd Prov. Light Inf. Regt. (2)
29th Light Inf. Regt. (2)
136th Line Inf. Regt. (4)

2nd Brigade Grillot
138th Line Inf. Regt. (4)
145th Line Inf. Regt. (4)

2 foot batteries (8 each)

10TH DIVISION:
GD Albert

1st Brigade Goris
4th Prov. Light Inf. Regt. (2)
139th Line Inf. Regt. (4)

2nd Brigade van Dedem
140th Line Inf. Regt. (4)
141st Line Inf. Regt. (4)

2 foot batteries (8 each)

11TH DIVISION:
GD Baron Ricard
1st Brigade Tarayre
9th Light Inf. Regt. (2)
17th Prov. Line Inf. Regt. (2)
18th Prov. Line Inf. Regt. (2)

2nd Brigade Dumoulin
142nd Line Inf. Regt. (4)
144th Line Inf. Regt. (4)

2 foot batteries (8 each)

39TH DIVISION:
GD Count Marchand

1st Brigade von Stockhorn
1st Baden Inf. Regt. (1)
3rd Baden Inf. Regt. Grand Duke (2)

2nd Brigade Prince Emil of Hesse
1st Hessian Light Inf. Regt. (2)
Hessian Life Guard Regt. (2)
Hessian Guard Regt. (2)

1/2 Baden foot battery (4), 1 Hessian foot battery (8)

Brigade Laboissière
10th Hussar Regt. (4)
1st Baden Dragoon Regt. (3)

Reserve Artillery

7 foot batteries, 2 horse batteries (8 each).

V CORPS:
GD Count Lauriston

17TH DIVISION:
GD Baron Puthod

1st Brigade Vachot
146th Line Inf. Regt. (4)

2nd Brigade (?)
147th Line Inf. Regt. (4)

3rd Brigade Pastol
148th Line Regt. (4)

2 foot batteries (8 each)

18TH DIVISION:
GD Lagrange

1st Brigade Charrière
134th Line Inf. Regt. (2)
154th Line Inf. Regt. (4)

2nd Brigade Suden
155th Line Inf. Regt. (4)
3rd Foreign Regt. (Irish Legion) (2)

2 foot batteries (8 each)

19TH DIVISION:
GD Rochambeau

1st Brigade Viscount de Lacroix
135th Line Inf. Regt. (4)

2nd Brigade Longchamp
149th Line Inf. Regt. (4)

3rd Brigade Lafitte
150th Line Inf. Regt. (4)

2 foot batteries (8 each)

Artillery Reserve

Brigade Camas
3 foot batteries (8 each), 2 horse batteries (6 each)

VII CORPS:
GD Reynier

32ND DIVISION:
GD Durutte

1st Brigade Devaux
35th Light Inf. Regt. (1 coy)
36th Light Inf. Regt. (1)
132nd Line Inf. Regt. (1)

2nd Brigade Jarry (absent)
133rd Line Regt. (1)
Würzburg Regt. (2)

ROYAL SAXON CORPS:
General von Zeschau

1st Brigade von Steindel (absent)
1st (Saxon) Light Inf. Regt. (1)
Guard Grenadiers (1)
Inf. Regt. Prince Frederick (1)
Inf. Regt. Steindel (1)

2nd Brigade von Sahr
2nd (Saxon) Light Inf. Regt. (1)
Amalgamated Grenadier Battalion
Amalgamated Inf. Regt. (2)

Light Cavalry (2)

1 foot battery, 1 horse battery (6 each)

BELOW **The remnants of the Grande Armée limped back through Germany at the beginning of 1813. Germans showed a mixture of pity and contempt for Napoleon's soldiers. It must however have been clear to all that Napoleon's power in Central Europe had been greatly diminished. (G. Lebrecht)**

THE RUSSIAN ARMY

The Russian Army had also suffered severely in the Campaign of 1812. It had endured the same climatic conditions as the Grande Armée and had hardly fared better when it came to supplies. Those Russian soldiers who had survived 1812 were hardy veterans indeed. On crossing the Vistula in February 1813, they numbered in total around 110,000 men. Of these, 70,000 were infantry in 150 regiments; 30,000 regular cavalry and Cossacks; 10,000 gunners with 849 guns.

Detachments were made to observe and besiege the various French-held fortresses and substantial forces were deployed to occupy an ever-rebellious Poland and observe Poniatowski, who was endeavouring to raise Polish forces to fight under Napoleon. That left a Main Army (1st Main Column) of around 33,700 men, 7,500 Cossacks and 280 guns that could support the Prussians in the field. As most of the Cossacks were irregulars, their numbers are given separately from the line troops.

Most infantry regiments had been reduced to a single battalion in strength. Most battalions consisted of little more than 350 men, and often less. Most cavalry regiments numbered only four squadrons instead of the regulation eight. Most squadrons counted less than 100 men.

The Russian forces were organised as follows:

Formation	Commander	Strength
1ˢᵗ Main Column	Wittgenstein	
Vanguard and other detachments		8,500 men, 28 guns
I Corps	Steinheil	7,000 men, 4 batteries
II Corps	Berg	5,000 men, 3 batteries
Reserve Corps	Fock	5,500 men, 18 guns
Various Detachments		7,700 men, parts of 3 batteries
Total		33,700 men, 189 guns
2ⁿᵈ Main Column	Platov	7,500 Cossacks, 2 batteries
3ʳᵈ Main Column	Chichagov	
Vanguard	Tchaplitz	
I Corps	Langeron	
II Corps	Voinov	
Cavalry Corps	Sass	
Total		9,900 infantry, 4,600 cavalry, 1,350 gunners, 9 batteries
4ᵗʰ Main Column	Kutusov	
Main Body	Tarmassov	
III Infantry (Grenadier) Corps	Kanovnizin	
V Infantry Corps (Guards)	Lavrov	
Cavalry Corps	Grand Prince Constantine	
Total		9,600 infantry, 4,950 cavalry, 2,550 gunners, 14 batteries
5ᵗʰ Main Column	Miloradovich	
Various Detachments		
IV Corps	Choglikov	
Infantry Corps	Prince Volchonsky	
Cavalry	Baron Korff	
Sub-total		6,000 infantry, 4,200 cavalry, 1,350 gunners, 9 batteries

Wintzingerode's Corps: 4,800 infantry, 3,900 cavalry, 900 gunners, 6 batteries
Sacken's Corps: 3,200 infantry, 2,200 cavalry, 600 gunners, 4 batteries
Dochterov's Corps: 6,000 infantry, 1,250 cavalry, 600 gunners, 4 batteries
Radt's Corps: 1,600 infantry, 800 cavalry, 600 gunners, 4 batteries
Total: 21,600 infantry, 12,350 cavalry, 4,050 gunners, 27 batteries

Total Russian forces: 112,500 men, 849 guns.

Napoleon at a graduation ceremony at the St Cyr military academy, spring 1813. He showed tireless energy in raising a new army to replace that lost in 1812. It is a tribute to his organisational skills that he was able to enter the contest for hegemony in Central Europe so quickly.

Reinforcements were certainly on their way, but due to the huge distances between their depots and the theatre of operations, these were not in a position to play a role in the combats of that spring.

There were three types of infantry in the Russian Army, musketeers (line infantry), grenadiers (élite infantry) and Jäger (light infantry). Each regiment was supposed to consist of two battalions, but the army that entered Germany at the beginning of 1813 consisted of the remnants of that of 1812 and was consequently very much under strength. A number of field amalgamations had taken place in an attempt to alleviate this situation. A variety of muskets and carbines were issued to the infantry. Captured French stocks were also used and supplies were received from Britain. As with all armies in this period, the great mixture of weaponry was a quartermaster's nightmare.

There were both heavy and light cavalry in the Russian Army. The heavy cavalry consisted of armoured cuirassiers and dragoons. The light cavalry consisted of hussars, chasseurs à cheval and uhlans (lancers). In addition, there was a large number of irregular Cossack formations attached to the army. Certain Cossack regiments were of a quality which allowed them to be considered regular formations.

Russian artillery batteries normally contained twelve pieces. 'Position' batteries contained 12-pdr, light and horse batteries 6-pdrs. Russian batteries also included 'licornes', a type of howitzer that fired shells over longer ranges at a flatter trajectory.

The Russian guard contained a number of élite infantry and cavalry regiments as well as Cossacks. It also had its own artillery.

THE PRUSSIAN ARMY

The Prussian Army had undergone a series of reforms from the end of Frederick the Great's reign onwards. The catastrophic defeats at Jena and Auerstadt in 1806 had focused attention on the need to continue this painful process through to its end. One of the stipulations of the

Marshal Michel Ney, Duke of Elchingen, Prince of the Moskwa, Bravest of the Brave. Ney is often blamed for Napoleon's failures in this campaign, particularly for being surprised at Grossgörschen and for delays in the flanking move at Bautzen. However, Napoleon was well aware that Ney had not posted scouts around his camp at Grossgörschen and also failed to communicate his plan to Ney at Bautzen, and so must carry some of the blame for the results.

peace treaty between Prussia and France after the Campaigns of 1806 and 1807 was that the size of the Prussian Army be restricted to 42,000 men. In 1806, the Prussian Army had numbered over 200,000 men. Mainly because of a general lack of funds at this time and partly as an attempt to overcome these restrictions, Prussia had developed the so-called 'Krümper' System. Under this system, new recruits were brought into the army, replacing trained soldiers. The latter were placed on furlough, with the new recruits then being trained in their place. By this method, a reserve of trained soldiers was established. These, together with the regular army, formed the core around which the national uprising of 1813 occurred. This core consisted of 33,000 infantry of relatively high quality, 12,000 well-trained cavalry and 6,000 gunners, as well as various fortress garrisons and engineer units. This total of 56,000 men was the nucleus around which the Prussian Army of 1813 expanded to meet this national emergency.

By calling up the reserves established through the Krümper System, a further 41,600 men were available to form 52 reserve battalions of infantry. Experienced officers who had been placed on half-pay in 1807 led these battalions. Volunteers from the middle classes who provided their own uniforms and equipment, along with so-called National Cavalry Regiments and Freikorps then augmented the army. A militia ('Landwehr') was called into being by a Royal Decree of 17 March 1813. This militia did not start to play an effective role in the hostilities until the autumn of 1813.

At the beginning of hostilities those Prussian formations ready to take the field included Yorck's Corps (19 battalions, 16 squadrons, 9 batteries, 3 sapper coys, 19,850 men, 72 guns), Bülow's Reserve Corps (11 battalions, 8 squadrons, 3 batteries, 10,600 men, 24 guns), Borstell's Pomeranian Brigade (4 battalions, 6 squadrons, 2 batteries, 1/2 sapper coy, 4,500 men, 16 guns), Blücher's Corps (The Royal Guard and those parts of the Brandenburg and Silesian Brigades that had not formed part of the Auxiliary Corps of 1812, 21 3/4 battalions, 42 squadrons, 12 1/2 batteries, 1 sapper coy, 28,300 men, 100 guns) and Lützow's Freikorps (1 battalion, 2 squadrons). By the end of March 1813, the field army consisted of around 65,000 men and 212 guns.

Besides the field army were a number of second line formations with a total strength of 47,000 men and 60 guns. Of these, 15,000 men with 24 guns under Generals Tauentzien and Schuler were besieging Stettin and Glogau. The remainder joined the field army during the spring of 1813. Furthermore, there were 23,000 third line troops in the fortresses and depots. Their mobilisation was completed during the Spring Campaign. In total the Prussian Army raised around 135,000 men and 272 guns that fateful spring.

Following the post-Jena reforms, a Prussian infantry regiment now consisted of three battalions – two of musketeers (line infantry) and one of fusiliers (light infantry). The two companies of grenadiers were amalgamated with those of another regiment to form an independent grenadier battalion. The theoretical strength of a battalion was around 800 men. The preferred battlefield formation was the column by the centre with the men of the third rank providing the skirmish element. At brigade level, the fusilier battalions provided the skirmish element, a Prussian brigade being the equivalent of a division in most other armies.

ALLIED ARMY, 2 MAY 1813

RUSSIAN I CORPS:
LG von Berg

5TH INFANTRY DIVISION:
MG Luckow

1st Brigade MG Mesenzoff
Perm Inf. Regt. (2)
Sievesk Inf. Regt. (1)
Mohilev Inf. Regt. (2)
Kalouga Inf. Regt. (2)
Grand Princess Catherine's Battalion

From the 4th Infantry Division: MG von Helfreich

Tenguinsk Inf. Regt. (2)
Estonia Inf. Regt. (2)

5th Heavy Foot Battery (12)
27th Light Foot Battery (6)

AMALGAMATED INFANTRY DIVISION:
MG Kasatschowsky

INFANTRY

1st Brigade Brischinsky
5 combined reserve battalions of the 1st Grenadier Division

2nd Brigade Glaskow
4 combined grenadier battalions of the 5th and 14th Divisions
1 militia battalion

CAVALRY:
MG Alexeyeff

Mittau Dragoon Regt. (3)
Riga Dragoon Regt. (2)
1st Cossack regt.
1st Don Cossack Battery (6)

II RUSSIAN ARMY CORPS:
LG von Wintzingerode

II INFANTRY CORPS:
LG Duke Eugene of Württemberg

3RD INFANTRY DIVISION:
MG Prince Schachafskoi

1st Brigade Kapustin
Reval Inf. Regt. (1)
20th Jäger Regt. (2)
21st Jäger Regt. (1)

2nd Brigade von Wolff
Mourmansk Inf. Regt. (2)
Chernigov Inf. Regt. (2)
Prov. Jäger Regt. (1)

6th Light Foot Battery (6)

4TH INFANTRY DIVISION:
MG Pyschnitzki

1st Brigade Talysin
Volhynia Inf. Regt. (2)
Kremenchouk Inf. Regt. (2)

4th Jäger Regt. (2)

7th Light Foot Battery (12)

CAVALRY CORPS:
MG Prince Trubetzkoy

1st Brigade Lanskoi
Alexandria Hussar Regt. (8)
White Russian Hussar Regt. (6)
Sum Hussar Regt. (2)

2nd Brigade Pantschoulitschev
Chernigov Chasseur à Cheval Regt. (5)
New Russia Dragoon Regt. (5)
Combined Dragoon Regt. (4)

3rd Brigade von Knorring
Tartar Uhlan Regt. (8)
Lithuanian Uhlan Regt. (2)

Prince Obolenski
1st Regular Ukraine Cossack Regt. (5)
3rd Regular Ukraine Cossack Regt. (5)

Artillery

1st Horse Battery (2)
2nd Horse Battery (6)
3rd Horse Battery (11)
7th Horse Battery (12)
8th Horse Battery (11)

9 Cossack regts.

RUSSIAN MAIN ARMY

III INFANTRY (GRENADIER) CORPS:
LG Konovnizin

1ST GRENADIER DIVISION:
MG Sulima

1st Brigade Kniaschin
Arakcheyev Grenadier Regt. (1)
Ekaterinoslav Grenadier Regt. (1)

2nd Brigade Acht
Taurien Grenadier Regt. (1)
St. Petersburg Grenadier Regt. (1)

3rd Heavy Foot Battery (12)

2ND GRENADIER DIVISION
MG Zwilenief

1st Brigade Pissareff
Kiev Grenadier Regt. (1)
Moscow Grenadier Regt. (1)

2nd Brigade Golowin
Astrakhan Grenadier Regt. (1)
Fangoria Grenadier Regt. (1)

3rd Brigade Hesse
Lesser Russian Grenadier Regt. (1)
Siberian Grenadier Regt. (1)

32nd Heavy Foot Battery (12)

V INFANTRY (GUARD) CORPS:
LG Lavrov

1ST GUARD INFANTRY DIVISION:
MG von Rosen

1st Brigade Potemkin
Preobragenski Guard Regt. (2)
Semenovski Guard Regt. (2)

2nd Brigade Krapovitzky
Ismailov Guard Regt. (2)
Guard Jäger Regt. (2)

1st Guard Light Foot Battery (12)
2nd Guard Light Foot Battery (12)

2ND GUARD INFANTRY DIVISION:
MG Udom

1st Brigade Krischanovsky
Lithuanian Guard Regt. (2)
Finnish Guard Regt. (2)

2nd Brigade Scheltuchin II
Pavlov Guard Regt. (1)
Life Grenadier Regt. (1)

2nd Guard Heavy Battery (12)

GUARD LIGHT CAVALRY DIVISION:
MG Chalikov

1st Brigade Krischanovsky
Life Guard Hussar Regt. (4)
Life Guard Uhlan Regt. (4)

2nd Brigade Chicherin (?)
Life Guard Dragoon Regt. (4)
Life Guard Cossack Regt. (5)

CUIRASSIER CORPS:
LG Prince Gallizin II

1ST CUIRASSIER DIVISION:
MG Depreradovich

1st Brigade Arseniet
Chevalier Guards (4)
Horse Guard Regt. (4)

2nd Brigade von Rosen
Czar's Cuirassier Regt. (3)
Czarina's Cuirassier Regt. (3)

3rd Brigade Grekov
Astrakhan Cuirassier Regt. (3)
Ekaterinoslav Cuirassier Regt. (3)

1st Guard Horse Battery (8)
Guard heavy battery (12)

2ND CUIRASSIER DIVISION:
GM Duka

1st Brigade Leontiev
Gluchov Cuirassier Regt. (3)
Pskov Cuirassier Regt. (3)

2nd Brigade Gudovich
Cuirassier Regt. of the Military Order (3)

3rd Brigade Massalov
Lesser Russian Cuirassier Regt. (3)
Novgorod Cuirassier Regt. (3)

2nd Guard Horse Battery (8)

Reserve Artillery MG Enter

3 heavy foot batteries (12 each)
1 light foot battery (12)

PRUSSIAN I ARMY CORPS:
General der Kavallerie von Blücher

Brandenburg Brigade:
MG von Roeder

Infantry: Oberst von Tippelskirch

Foot Guard Regt. (3)
Normal Battalion (1)
Combined Volunteer Jäger Battalion (formed from the four detachments of the Foot Guards and Normal Battalion)
Guard Jäger Battalion
Life Grenadier Battalion
1st East Prussian Grenadier Battalion
III Battalion, Life Regt.

Cavalry: Oberstlt. von Katzler

Brandenburg Hussar Regt. (2)
West Prussian Uhlan Regt. (4)

6-pdr. Foot Battery No. 4 (Guard) (8)
6-pdr. Foot Battery No. 9 (8)
Horse Battery No. 8 (Guard) (8)

Lower Silesian Brigade:
Oberst von Klüx

Infantry: Major von Jagow

1st West Prussian Infantry Regt. (3)
2nd West Prussian Infantry Regt. (2)
West Prussian Grenadier Battalion
Silesian Schützen Battalion (2 coys)

Cavalry: Oberst von Mutius

1st West Prussian Dragoon Regt. (2)
Silesian Uhlan Regt. (2)

6-pdr Foot Battery No.7 (8)
6-pdr Foot Battery No.8 (8)
Horse Battery No.7 (8)

Upper Silesian Brigade

Infantry: Oberst von Pirch I

1st Silesian Infantry Regt. (3)
2nd Silesian Infantry Regt. (2)
Silesian Grenadier Battalion
Silesian Schützen Battalion (2 coys)

Cavalry: Major Laroche von Starkenfels
Neumark Dragoon Regt. (4)
1st Silesian Hussar Regt. (2)
2nd Silesian Hussar Regt. (2)

6-pdr Foot Battery No.11 (8)
6-pdr Foot Battery No.13 (8)
Horse Battery No.9 (8)

Reserve Cavalry: Oberst von Dolffs
Gardes du Corps Regt. (4)
Guard Light Cavalry Regt. (4)
Silesian Cuirassier Regt. (4)
East Prussian Cuirassier Regt. (4)

Brandenburg Cuirassier Regt. (4)
Guard Volunteer Cossacks (1)
Guard Volunteer Jäger (1)

Horse Battery No.4 (8)
Horse Battery No.10 (8)

Reserve Artillery: Oberst von Braun

1/2 12-pdr. Foot Battery No.3 (4)

PRUSSIAN II ARMY CORPS:
LG von Yorck

Brigade GM von Hünerbein
1st East Prussian Infantry Regt. (3)
Fusilier Battalion / Life Regt.
Lithuanian Dragoon Regt. (4)
6-pdr Foot Battery No.1

Brigade Oberst von Horn
2nd West Prussian Infantry Regt. (2)
2nd Silesian Infantry Regt. (2)
II Battalion / 1st Silesian Infantry Regt.
(2nd) Combined Dragoon Regt. (4)
6-pdr Foot Battery No.2 (8)
1/2 12-pdr Foot Battery No.3 (4)

Brigade Oberstlt. von Steinmetz
Colberg Infantry Regt. (3)
2nd Life Hussar Regt. (4)
1/2 3-pdr Foot Battery (4)
Horse Battery No.2 (8)
Horse Battery No.3 (8) (Attached to Blücher's Reserve Cavalry on 2 May 1813)

DEFENDING LEIPZIG:

PRUSSO-RUSSIAN ARMY CORPS:
LG von Kleist

PRUSSIANS:

Life Infantry Regt. (2)
I Battalion / 1st West Prussian Infantry Regt.
Fusilier Battalion / 2nd East Prussian Infantry Regt.
East Prussian Jäger Battalion (2 coys)
Combined Hussar Regt. (4)
6-pdr Foot Battery No.3 (8)
1/2 3-pdr Foot Battery (4)
Horse Battery No.1 (8)

RUSSIANS:
MG von Roth

Jäger Regt. No.23 (2)
Jäger Regt. No.24 (2)
Jäger Regt. No.25 (2)
Jäger Regt. No.26 (2)
Grodno Hussar Regt. (6)
3 Regts of Cossacks
1 Heavy Foot Battery (10)
1/2 Horse Battery (6) (on 2 May 1813, three guns were attached to Berg's Corps, three to Blücher's)

ALLIED ARMY 20–21 MAY 1813

LEFT WING UNDER GENERAL MILORADOVICH

Detachments on the far left flank:

Detachment of MG Kaissarov
10th Don Cossack Regt.
1st Bashkir Regt.
Various detachments of Cossacks
Neumark Dragoons (1)

Detachment of MG Emanuel
Kharkov Dragoon Regt. (3)
Kiev Dragoon Regt. (3)
Various detachments of Cossacks
4th Horse Battery (6)

Detachment of MG Loukov
2 battalions (probably from 5th Division), 2 guns.

UNDER GL PRINCE GORSCHAKOV II:

17TH INFANTRY DIVISION

Brest Regt. (1)
Riazan Regt. (1)
Bielozersk Regt. (1)
4th Jäger Regt. (1)

1 heavy battery, taken from the Artillery Reserve (12)

Infantry Reserve ad hoc
2nd Brigade of 2nd Division Scheltuchin II
Life Regt. (1)
Pavlov Regt. (1)

Cavalry Brigade Lissanievich
Akhtyrsk Hussar Regt. (3)
Chogouiev Uhlan Regt. (3)
Kargopolo Dragoon Regt. (3)

1/2 3rd Horse Battery (6)

GUARD LIGHT CAVALRY DIVISION:
GM Chalikov

1st Brigade Krichanovski
Life Guard Hussar Regt. (4)
Life Guard Uhlan Regt. (4)

2nd Brigade Chicherin (?)
Life Guard Dragoon Regt. (4)
Life Guard Cossack Regt. (2)

UNDER THE COMMAND OF LG COUNT OSTERMANN-TOLSTOI

Infantry

II INFANTRY CORPS:
LG Duke Eugene of Württemberg

3RD INFANTRY DIVISION:
MG Prince Schachafskoi

1st Brigade Kapustin
Reval Inf. Regt. (1)
20th Jäger Regt. (2)
21st Jäger Regt. (1)

2nd Brigade von Wolff
Mourm Inf. Regt. (2)
Chernigov Inf. Regt. (2)

4TH INFANTRY DIVISION:
MG Saint-Priest

1st Brigade Talysin
Tobolsk Inf. Regt. (2)
4th Jäger Regt. (2)
34th Jäger Regt. (1)

2nd Brigade Treffurt
Volhynia Inf. Regt. (2)
Kremenchouk Inf. Regt. (2)
Riga Inf. Regt. (1)

33rd Light Artillery Battery (12)
1st Heavy Artillery Battery (12)
Heavy artillery battery (8) (from Reserve)

IV INFANTRY CORPS:
GL Markov I

11TH INFANTRY DIVISION:
GM Karpenkov

1st Brigade
Yelets Inf. Regt. (1)
1st Jäger Regt. (1)
33rd Jäger Regt. (2)

2nd Brigade (ad hoc)
Koporsk Inf. Regt. (1) (from 3rd Division)
Staroskol Inf. Regt. (2) (from 22nd Division)

Artillery
44th Light Battery (6)

8TH INFANTRY DIVISION:
GM Engelhardt
Archangel Inf. Regt. (1)
Schlüsselburg Inf. Regt. (1)
Old Ingrie Inf. Regt. (1)

27th Light Artillery Battery (12)

INFANTRY DIVISION AD HOC:
MG Saint-Priest

1st Brigade (from 22nd Division)
Viatka Inf. Regt. (2)
Olonetz Inf. Regt. (1)

2nd Brigade
11th Jäger Regt. (2) (from 7th Division)
37th Jäger Regt. (1) (from 8th Division)

3rd Light Artillery Battery (12)

Cavalry Brigade von Knorring
Soum Hussar Regt. (4)
Tartar Regt. (4)
Combined Dragoon Regt. (1)

1/2 7th Horse Artillery Battery (6)

Cossack Brigade Prince Obolenski
1st Ukraine Cossack Regt.
3rd Ukraine Cossack Regt.

Cavalry Brigade Mellissio
Loubno Hussar Regt. (3)
Moscow Dragoon Regt. (3)
Mittau Dragoon Regt. (3)

1/2 3rd Horse Artillery Battery (6)

UNDER THE COMMAND OF LG BERG

5TH INFANTRY DIVISION:
MG Luckow

1st Brigade Kalachowsky
Perm Inf. Regt. (2)
Mohilev Inf. Regt. (2)

2nd Brigade Prince of Siberia
Sievesk Inf. Regt. (1)
Kalouga Inf. Regt. (2)
Grand Princess Catherine's Battalion

FROM THE 4TH INFANTRY DIVISION:
MG von Helfreich

1st Brigade Mesenzoff
Tenguinsk Inf. Regt. (2)
Estonia Inf. Regt. (2)

13th Light Foot Battery (10)
5th Heavy Foot Battery (12)
14th Heavy Foot Battery (12)

Cavalry Brigade Pantschoulitschev
Chernigov Chasseur à Cheval Regt. (3)
New Russian Dragoon Regt. (3)
Lithuanian Uhlan Regt. (2)

1/2 7th Horse Artillery Battery (6)

RUSSIAN RESERVES
Grand Duke Constantine

III INFANTRY CORPS (GRENADIERS):
GL Raiewski

1ST GRENADIER DIVISION:
GM Soulima
Count Arakcheiev's Grenadier Regt. (1)
Ekaterinoslav Grenadier Regt. (1)
St. Petersburg Grenadier Regt. (1)
Tauride Grenadier Regt. (1)
Pernau Grenadier Regt. (1)
Kexholm Grenadier Regt. (1)
Combined Grenadier Battalions of 5th and 14th Divisions (4)

14th Light Foot Battery (12)
36th Light Foot Battery (12)
3rd Heavy Foot Battery (12)

2ND GRENADIER DIVISION:
GM Zwilenieff
Kiev Grenadier Regt. (1)
Moscow Grenadier Regt. (1)
Astrakhan Grenadier Regt. (1)
Fangoria Grenadier Regt. (1)
Lesser Russian Grenadier Regt. (1)
Siberian Grenadier Regt. (1)

32nd Heavy Foot Battery (12)
39th Heavy Foot Battery (8)

V INFANTRY (GUARD) CORPS:
LG Lavrov

1ST GUARD INFANTRY DIVISION:
MG von Rosen

1st Brigade Potemkin
Preobragenski Guard Regt. (2)
Semenovski Guard Regt. (2)

2nd Brigade Krapowitzky
Ismailov Guard Regt. (2)
Guard Jäger Regt. (2)

2ND GUARD INFANTRY DIVISION:
LG Count Yermolov

1st Brigade Kritschanowsky
Lithuanian Guard Regt. (2)
Finnish Guard Regt. (2)

2nd Brigade Scheltuchin II
Pavlov Guard Regt. (1)
Life Grenadier Regt. (1)

1st Guard Heavy Battery (12)
2nd Guard Heavy Battery (12)
1st Guard Light Foot Battery (12)
2nd Guard Light Foot Battery (12)
1st Guard Horse Battery (8)
2nd Guard Horse Battery (6)

CUIRASSIER CORPS:
LG Ouvarov

1ST CUIRASSIER DIVISION:
MG Depreradovich

1st Brigade Arseniev
Chevalier Guards (4)
Horse Guard Regt. (4)

2nd Brigade von Rosen
Czar's Cuirassier Regt. (3)
Czarina's Cuirassier Regt. (3)

3rd Brigade Grekov
Astrakhan Cuirassier Regt. (3)
Ekaterinoslav Cuirassier Regt. (3)

2ND CUIRASSIER DIVISION:
GM Duka

1st Brigade Leontiev
Gluchov Cuirassier Regt. (3)
Pskov Cuirassier Regt. (3)

2nd Brigade Gudovich
Cuirassier Regt. of the Military Order (3)

3rd Brigade Massalov
Lesser Russian Cuirassier Regt. (3)
Novgorod Cuirassier Regt. (3)

RESERVE ARTILLERY:
MG Enter

2nd Heavy Foot Battery (10)
7th Heavy Foot Battery (12)
30th Heavy Foot Battery (6)
31st Heavy Foot Battery (12)
33rd Heavy Foot Battery (12)
6th Light Foot Battery (12)
7th Light Foot Battery (12)
32nd Light Foot Battery (12)
42nd Light Foot Battery (12)

1st Horse Battery (2)
6th Horse Battery (6)
8th Horse Battery (6)
10th Horse Battery (6)
23rd Horse Battery (6)

PRUSSIAN ARMY:
General der Kavallerie von Blücher

I ARMY CORPS:
General von Yorck

Brigade Oberstlt. von Steinmetz
1st East Prussian Inf. Regt. (2)
Life Regt. (2)
Combined Fusilier Battalion 1st East
Prussians/Life

Brigade Oberst von Horn
I Battalion / 1st West Prussian Inf. Regt.
I Battalion / 2nd West Prussian Inf. Regt.
II Battalion / 1st Silesian Inf. Regt.
II Battalion / 2nd Silesian Inf. Regt.
Combined Fusilier Battalion of 2nd West
Prussians / 2nd Silesians

Cavalry Brigade GM von Corswandt
Lithuanian Dragoon Regt. (4)
1st West Prussian Dragoon Regt. (4)
Combined Silesian Hussar Regt. (4)

Artillery

1/2 12-pdr Foot Battery No. 3 (4)
6-pdr Foot Battery No. 1 (8)
6-pdr Foot Battery No. 2 (8)
6-pdr Horse Battery No. 2 (8)
6-pdr Horse Battery No. 3 (8)

II ARMY CORPS:
General der Kavallerie von Blücher

Lower Silesian Brigade Oberst von Klüx
West Prussian Grenadier Battalion
1st East Prussian Inf. Regt. (3)
2nd East Prussian Inf. Regt. (2)
Life Regt. (1)
Silesian Schützen Battalion (2 coys)

Cavalry
Silesian Uhlan Regt. (2)
Brandenburg Dragoon Regt. (2)

Artillery
6-pdr Foot Battery No.7 (8)
6-pdr Foot Battery No.8 (8)
Horse Battery No.7 (8)

Upper Silesian Brigade:
GM von Zieten
Silesian Grenadier Battalion
1st Silesian Infantry Regt. (3)
2nd Silesian Infantry Regt. (2)
Life Regt. (1)
Silesian Schützen Battalion (2 coys)

Cavalry
Neumark Dragoon Regt. (4)
1st Silesian Hussar Regt. (2)
2nd Silesian Hussar Regt. (2)

6-pdr Foot Battery No.11 (8)
6-pdr Foot Battery No.13 (8)
Horse Battery No.9 (7)

Brandenburg Brigade:
GM von Roeder
Foot Guard Regt. (3)
Normal Battalion
Combined Volunteer Jäger Battalion
Guard Jäger Battalion
Life Grenadier Battalion
1st East Prussian Grenadier Battalion
III Battalion, Life Regt.

Cavalry
Brandenburg Hussar Regt. (4)
Brandenburg Uhlan Regt. (2)

Artillery
1/2 12-pdr Foot Battery No. 3 (Guard) (4)
6-pdr Foot Battery No. 1 (Guard) (8)
6-pdr Foot Battery No. 9 (8)
6-pdr Horse Battery No. 8 (Guard) (8)
6-pdr Horse Battery No. 9 (8)

RESERVE CAVALRY:
Oberst von Dolffs

1st Brigade Oberstlt. von Werder
Gardes du Corps Regt. (4)
Guard Light Cavalry Regt. (4)
Guard Volunteer Cossacks (1)
Guard Volunteer Jäger (1)
6-pdr Horse Battery No. 4 (Guard) (8)

2nd Brigade Oberst von Jürgass
Silesian Cuirassier Regt. (4)
East Prussian Cuirassier Regt. (4)
Brandenburg Cuirassier Regt. (4)
Horse Battery No.10 (8)

Reserve Artillery (ad hoc) (Russians)
1st Guard Heavy Foot Battery (12)
2 heavy foot batteries (12 each)
1 light foot battery (12)

PRUSSO-RUSSIAN ARMY CORPS:
LG von Kleist

Prussian Brigade
Colberg Regt. (3)
Fusilier Battalion / 2nd East Prussian Inf. Regt.
East Prussian Jäger Battalion (2 coys)
2nd Life Hussar Regt. (4)
6-pdr Foot Battery No.3 (8)
1/2 3-pdr Foot Battery (4)
Horse Battery No.1 (8)

Russian Brigade Roth:
(taken from 5th and 14th Inf. Divisions)
23rd Jäger Regt. (1)
24th Jäger Regt. (1)
25th Jäger Regt. (1)
26th Jäger Regt. (1)
Grodno Hussar Regt. (4)
3 Cossack Regts.
21st Heavy Foot Battery (9)
23rd Horse Battery (6)

CORPS OF GENERAL BARCLAY DE TOLLY:

VANGUARD:
LG Tchaplitz

Infantry (from 13th Inf. Division)
12th Jäger Regt. (1)
22nd Jäger Regt. (1)

Cavalry
Olviopol Hussar Regt. (2)
Jitomir Uhlan Regt. (2)
3 regts. Cossacks
34th Light Foot Battery (12)

MAIN CORPS:
General Langeron

1st Brigade ad hoc MG Prince Schtscherbatov
Tambov Inf. Regt. (1)
Vladimir Inf. Regt. (1)
Dniepr Inf. Regt. (1)
Kostroma Inf. Regt. (1)
28th Jäger Regt. (1)
32nd Jäger Regt. (1)
Kinburn Dragoon Regt. (2)
Jitomir Chasseur à Cheval Regt. (2)
35th Light Foot Battery (12)

2nd Brigade ad hoc MG Jukow
Yakutsk Inf. Regt. (1)
Nacheburg Inf. Regt. (1)
10th Jäger Regt. (1)
7th Jäger Regt. (1)
Tver Dragoon Regt. (2)
Dorpat Chasseur à Cheval Regt. (2)
35th Light Foot Battery (12)

RESERVE:
MG Sass
Vitebsk Inf. Regt. (1)
Koslov Inf. Regt. (1)
Koura Inf. Regt. (1)
Kolyvan Inf. Regt. (1)
Arassmas Chasseur à Cheval Regt. (1)
1 regt. Cossacks
15th Heavy Foot Battery (12)
18th Heavy Foot Battery (12)
34th Heavy Foot Battery (12)
29th Light Foot Battery (12)

MOBILE CORPS:
MG Lanskoy

Alexandria Hussar Regt. (3)
White Russian Hussar Regt. (3)
Livonian Chasseur à Cheval Regt. (3)
7 Cossack regts.
2nd Horse Artillery Battery (6)

MOBILE CORPS:
Figner

2 Cossack regts.
2nd Horse Artillery Battery (2)

Henri-Gratien Bertrand who commanded the French IV Corps at both Lützen and Bautzen.

Armament consisted of a variety of muskets, both foreign patterns and various patterns manufactured domestically. The former included weapons either obtained from abroad, particularly Austrian, British and Russian patterns, or captured patterns, particularly the French Charleville musket. The latter included the 1787 pattern, normally used with a modified butt, the 1805 pattern or Nothardt musket, the 1809 pattern or New Prussian musket. The myriad small arms were a quarter-master's nightmare, but in the disruption caused by such a long period of warfare this was almost inevitable.

The cavalry consisted of heavy cavalry known as cuirassiers, medium cavalry known as dragoons and light cavalry divided into hussars and lance-armed uhlans. Unlike particularly the French cuirassiers, the Prussian heavies did not wear body-armour. They were armed with a straight sword, as were the dragoons. The hussars carried the traditional curved sabre. All troopers carried a brace of pistols and a number of men were armed with carbines to be used in skirmishing and when on picket duty. Each regiment consisted of four squadrons.

The artillery was organised into batteries of eight pieces, normally six cannon and two howitzers. The foot artillery consisted of heavy, 12-pdr cannon and 10-pdr howitzers, and light, 6-pdr cannon with 7-pdr howitzers. The horse artillery used the lighter pieces.

The British Contribution

On the outbreak of hostilities in Central Europe, Britain already had a military commitment in Spain. This consisted of an Expeditionary Force under the Duke of Wellington. Furthermore, Britain had a military commitment to its colonial empire. Although the most developed economy in Europe at this time, Britain was unable to provide more manpower for a further military intervention on the Continent of Europe. Instead, Britain provided its allies in the Central European theatre with supplies and subventions – guineas and gunpowder. That spring, the workshop of the world provided the Prussians and Russians with around 200,000 muskets along with accoutrements and flints, 116 cannon and 1,200 tons of ammunition. These supplies were shipped to ports in Northern Germany. Much of this material did not reach the front line formations until the summer of 1813, that is, after the cease-fire.

OPPOSING PLANS

Napoleon conceived a four-phase plan to resolve the crisis in Germany. Firstly, he would retain control of as much of Germany as he could with the forces immediately available. Secondly, using these forces he would buy time to allow his new army to assemble in France. Once this was achieved he would march at the head of this army to re-establish control over Germany. Finally, he would restore contact with his isolated fortress garrisons, regaining his position as master of Central Europe. Every success along the road would help persuade his now reluctant allies to toe the line.

The Prusso-Russian forces aimed to buy enough time to allow Russian reinforcements to arrive and strengthen the Allies' position. The hope was that this would also spark an uprising across Northern Germany, causing Napoleon further problems. Finally the time won would allow negotiations to take place with the Austrians. Persuading the forces of the Habsburg crown to join the new coalition would probably tip the scales decisively in the Allies' favour. But to persuade the Emperor to join the struggle against Napoleon, the Prusso-Russian forces would have to show themselves capable of matching the French on the field of battle.

The Theatre of Operations

This campaign was fought largely in Poland and the eastern part of Germany. Three main rivers cross this area, running roughly north to south. These are, from east to west, the Vistula, the Oder and the Elbe. Four major fortresses controlled the line of the Vistula – Danzig, Graudenz, Thorn and Modlin. Of these, all but Graudenz were in French hands. The three key fortresses along the River Oder, Stettin, Küstrin and Glogau, were all in French hands. The line of the River Elbe was held by fortresses at Madgeburg, Wittenberg and Torgau. The French garrisoned the first two, the uncommitted Saxons the third. The French also held the fortress of Spandau, near Berlin. Posen, the city where Eugène de Beauharnais first attempted to form an army to halt the Russian advance, lay halfway between the Vistula and the Oder.

These rivers and their fortified crossing points were the only appreciable physical barriers across the North German Plain over which the armies marched. With most of the fortresses and crossings in their hands, the French clearly held an advantage. However, the population of Prussia was a seething mass of resentment with a strong desire to avenge the humiliations of 1806. It would take little to ignite a rebellion against the French. This presented a clear threat to the French lines of communication. It was far from certain how long the French would be able to maintain their hold on the river crossings and fortresses.

East Prussia was already in a state of open rebellion – against both its king and Napoleon. Poland, allied to the French and very sympathetic to

The Prince of Sayn-Wittgenstein, Russian general and Allied commander in the spring of 1813. As with so many Russian officers, Wittgenstein was of German origins. His performance in the Spring Campaign was considered inadequate and Barclay de Tolly replaced him.

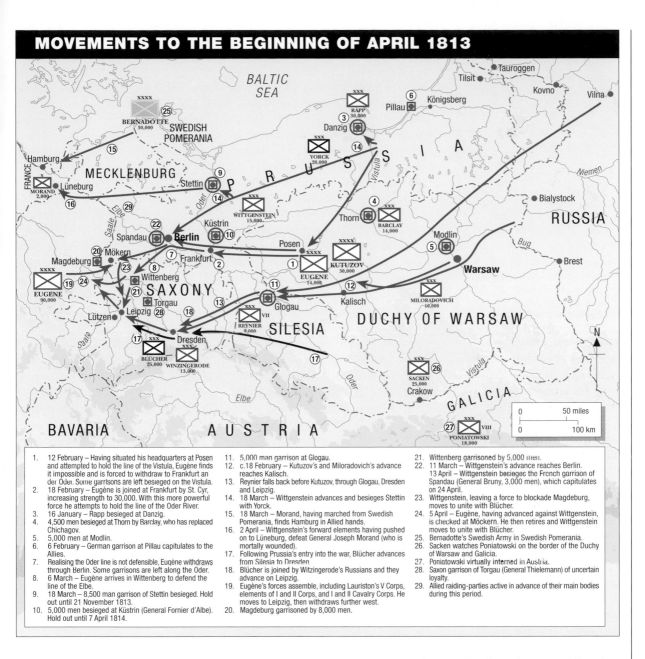

1. 12 February – Having situated his headquarters at Posen and attempted to hold the line of the Vistula, Eugène finds it impossible and is forced to withdraw to Frankfurt on der Oder. Some garrisons are left besieged on the Vistula.
2. 18 February – Eugène is joined at Frankfurt by St. Cyr, increasing strength to 30,000. With this more powerful force he attempts to hold the line of the Oder River.
3. 16 January – Rapp besieged at Danzig.
4. 4,500 men besieged at Thorn by Barclay, who has replaced Chichagov.
5. 5,000 men at Modlin.
6. 6 February – German garrison at Pillau capitulates to the Allies.
7. Realising the Oder line is not defensible, Eugène withdraws through Berlin. Some garrisons are left along the Oder.
8. 6 March – Eugène arrives in Wittenberg to defend the line of the Elbe.
9. 18 March – 8,500 man garrison of Stettin besieged. Hold out until 21 November 1813.
10. 5,000 men besieged at Küstrin (General Fornier d'Albe). Hold out until 7 April 1814.
11. 5,000 man garrison at Glogau.
12. c.18 February – Kutuzov's and Miloradovich's advance reaches Kalisch.
13. Reynier falls back before Kutuzov, through Glogau, Dresden and Leipzig.
14. 18 March – Wittgenstein advances and besieges Stettin with Yorck.
15. 18 March – Morand, having marched from Swedish Pomerania, finds Hamburg in Allied hands.
16. 2 April – Wittgenstein's forward elements having pushed on to Lüneburg, defeat General Joseph Morand (who is mortally wounded).
17. Following Prussia's entry into the war, Blücher advances from Silesia to Dresden.
18. Blücher is joined by Witzingerode's Russians and they advance on Leipzig.
19. Eugène's forces assemble, including Lauriston's V Corps, elements of I and II Corps, and I and II Cavalry Corps. He moves to Leipzig, then withdraws further west.
20. Magdeburg garrisoned by 8,000 men.
21. Wittenberg garrisoned by 5,000 men.
22. 11 March – Wittgenstein's advance reaches Berlin. 13 April – Wittgenstein besieges the French garrison of Spandau (General Bruny, 3,000 men), which capitulates on 24 April.
23. Wittgenstein, leaving a force to blockade Magdeburg, moves to unite with Blücher.
24. 5 April – Eugène, having advanced against Wittgenstein, is checked at Möckern. He then retires and Wittgenstein moves to unite with Blücher.
25. Bernadotte's Swedish Army in Swedish Pomerania.
26. Sacken watches Poniatowski on the border of the Duchy of Warsaw and Galicia.
27. Poniatowski virtually interned in Austria.
28. Saxon garrison of Torgau (General Thielemann) of uncertain loyalty.
29. Allied raiding-parties active in advance of their main bodies during this period.

the Bonapartist cause, was in a state of turmoil. The advance of Russian forces would extinguish that country's independence for more than a century. Prussia, nominally an ally of France, was clearly awaiting an opportunity to switch sides. This would cut off the French-garrisoned fortresses and deny much of Eastern Germany to Napoleon. The Prussian province of Silesia, in the south-east of the kingdom, was a natural base of operations for a Russian advance into Central Germany, and it was to here the Prussians transferred their seat of government.

The Opening Moves

On 17 January 1813, Napoleon placed his troops in Germany under the command of Viceroy Eugène de Beauharnais. Eugène did his best to rally the scattered remains of the Grande Armée of 1812 in the Polish

General Barclay de Tolly. A Russian general of Scottish origins, he succeeded Wittgenstein as Allied commander after the Battle of Bautzen. By then, it was too late for him to play a significant role in the outcome of the campaign.

Prince Kutusov. Seen as the liberator of the Motherland in 1812, he was reluctant to see the Russian Army get involved in the struggle for Central Europe. This reluctance hindered the Russian advance into Germany and allowed Napoleon time to rebuild his forces. Had Kutusov acted more decisively, Napoleon may well have lost control of all of Germany before he had raised a new army.

town of Posen. He had at his disposal 4,000 men in each of the fortresses of Modlin and Zamosc. In Danzig (Gdansk), he had 30,000 men and in Thorn (Torun) 4,500. His only reserve was the Division Lagrange together with Division Grenier, the latter on its way from Italy. These forces numbered a further 28,000 men.

Facing them were 11,000 Russians from Wittgenstein's forces who were advancing into Germany. Other forces moved to cut off the fortresses of Danzig and Thorn, breaching the first line of defence, along the Vistula River. The fortress of Pillau on the Baltic coast of East Prussia capitulated to the Allies on 6 February.

Misgivings over Austrian intentions led to a pause in the Russian advance. The movements of Field Marshal Prince Schwarzenberg's Corps, the Austrian contingent in the Grande Armée of 1812, across Poland had caused consternation. Austria, Russia and Prussia had partitioned Poland among themselves at the end of the 18th century, and all had territorial claims in the Polish state re-instituted by Napoleon. Schwarzenberg's men placed the Austrian statesman Metternich in a good position to play a role in mediating a peace in Europe. As Napoleon's forces had been crushed in Russia, the Prussian state virtually bankrupted by the French occupation and Russia's armed forces reduced to a pale shadow by the Campaign of 1812, the one sizeable force still intact was Schwarzenberg's. However, Austria felt that it would be better policy to extract his Corps from the chaos left in the wake of Napoleon's retreat.

Technically, the Austrians were still allies of Napoleon and at war with Russia, so negotiations for a cease-fire with the Russians commenced on 6 January. A few days later, the Russian advance into Poland recommenced. Not wanting to be seen to breach their alliance with Napoleon, the Austrians arranged for the Russian forces to move in such a way that Schwarzenberg was left with no choice but to withdraw. The Austrians evacuated Warsaw by 6 February, moving south. This made the position of Reynier's Saxon Corps untenable. Until then, the Saxons had been co-operating with the Austrians. Reynier fought his was back to Kalisch, south-west of Warsaw. On 25 February, the Austrians and Russians signed a cease-fire. The Russian westward advance could now continue unopposed.

The remains of four corps of the Grande Armée had been sent to garrison various fortresses, leaving Lagrange's Division, which had not yet reached Posen, Eugène's headquarters, for use in the field. Poniatowski's and Reynier's Corps had been checked by Russian moves, so all that was available in Posen were the remnants of the Guard, VI, VIII and IX Corps. Small numbers of reinforcements were moving to join Eugène. From the troops at his disposal Eugène formed four weak divisions under Roguet, Rechberg, Gérard and Girard. When Grenier's Division arrived from Italy at the end of January, it was divided in two and used to form a new XI Corps under Marshal St. Cyr.

The reports coming in of Prussian and Russian activity caused Eugène concern about his ability to hold a position so far forward. The uprising in East Prussia led by Yorck was one danger. Another came from the Russians, who had now negotiated a cease-fire with the Austrians. Then, on 3 February, the King of Prussia called for volunteers to join his army and moved his government from Berlin to Breslau. In Silesia he would be beyond the reach of French interference. Here was a signal if it were needed that Prussia was about to rise against Napoleon, threatening Eugène's line of communications. Russian raiding parties already hitting the French lines of communication deep inside Prussia further exacerbated Eugène's already precarious situation. On 12 February, the Viceroy started a withdrawal to Frankfort an der Oder, the bulk of his troops arriving there on 20 February. He was harrassed every step of the way by Cossack raiders.

Once Eugène had crossed the Oder River, his position improved significantly. With the additional manpower now available to him, he would be able to hold the bridgeheads across the Oder and turn it into a significant barrier. He now had about 50,000 men and 94 guns at his disposal. His right wing, the 9,000 men and 32 guns of Reynier's Corps, was stationed at Glogau, along with some Polish contingents. Rechberg's Bavarian Division was at Krossen – 2,300 men with 12 guns. Stationed along a line between Frankfort an der Oder and Küstrin were Roguet's, Girard's and Gerard's Divisions from Posen and Grenier's and Charpentier's Divisions (formed from Grenier's Division), a total of 35,000 men and 46 guns. A weak detachment of about 4,000 men and four guns, formed from the remains of I Corps and parts of the garrison of Stettin, held Schwedt. To their rear, forming the second line around Berlin, was Lagrange's Division, just reinforced to almost 14,000 men and 40 guns. A detachment of 3,000 men and 17 guns under General Morand was in Swedish Pomerania. In addition to these men were the increasing numbers of stragglers from Russia rejoining the army. At this time, 4,000 were in Glogau, 2,800 in Küstrin, 4,400 in Stettin and 1,300 in Spandau. Finally, there were about 7,000 wounded in Berlin and Frankfort an der Oder but their potential combat value was negligible.

Napoleon's new army was beginning to assemble on the Elbe. By the middle of March, he had 22,400 men with 34 guns forming the Corps of Observation of the Elbe. It later became V Corps under Lauriston. He had an additional 1,900 men in Erfurt. All were poorly trained and equipped however and could not be expected to support Eugène for some time. In this light Eugène decided to take a defensive stance along the Oder line, rather than the offensive posture Napoleon wished.

The Prusso-Russian Alliance

King Frederick William of Prussia left Berlin for Breslau on 22 January. A French garrison occupied the fortress of Spandau near Berlin and more of Napoleon's troops were moving into the Mark of Brandenburg, the Prussian province around Berlin. To contemplate going to war with an enemy occupying a substantial part of one's own territory is a risky business and Frederick William needed certain very clear assurances from the Russians before doing so. The negotiations with the Czar's representatives reached a conclusion with the signing of a treaty of alliance on 27 February. Prussia could now begin the preparations for war in earnest.

Meanwhile, Cossack raiding-parties under Czernichev, Tettenborn and Benckendorff crossed the River Oder near Küstrin and spread terror throughout the French-occupied areas. By 20 February, Czernichev and Tettenborn reached Berlin, where they demanded its surrender by its French commandant Augereau. Although the garrison chased off the Cossacks, the effect on morale was significant, striking fear into the French and encouraging the Prussians to stage an uprising.

General der Kavallerie Blücher. The symbol of anti-Bonapartism in Germany, Blücher was highly popular with his men. While he led from the front his chief-of-staff commanded the army, forming the dual leadership that came to characterise Prussian and later German armies.

A French Général de Division and his adjutant. The division was the standard grand tactical unit in the French Army of this period. Napoleon was fortunate to have a number of highly experienced and most capable men to fill this post. Watercoloured lithograph by Bellangé.

Concerned that his forces may become trapped in the Oder fortresses, Eugène now decided to abandon the line of the river. Before doing so, he blew up the bridges and removed all shipping. Two natural defence lines across this part of the North German Plain had now been abandoned to the Russians. Leaving Gérard for the time being in Frankfort an der Oder with 3,000 men and 8 guns, Eugène marched with Roguet's Division from Frankfort an der Oder via Fürstenwalde to Köpenick, reaching the outskirts of Berlin on 22 February. Girard's Division marched via Müncheberg and Fürstenwalde, as did Grenier and Charpentier, joining Eugène at Köpenick. The detachment at Schwedt was ordered to Stettin. In response to Augereau's urgent appeals for assistance, the Guard Cavalry, about 1,000 sabres, was sent off first. By the beginning of March, the French had concentrated about 29,000 men around Berlin.

Rechberg's Bavarians, now under Reynier's orders, fell back to Kalau via Guben and Cottbus. Reynier abandoned Glogau on 22 February, marching via Sprottau, Sagan and Rothenburg and reaching Bautzen on 1 March. From here he was ordered to fall back to Dresden and secure this important Elbe crossing.

The Russians had meanwhile halted their advance, partly as a result of the general exhaustion of their troops and partly due to delays in concluding the alliance with Prussia. At the beginning of March their advance resumed. Three raiding parties totalling 8,500 men and 24 guns moved on Berlin. This was enough to convince Eugène that he could no longer hold this city. Painfully aware of the implications of abandoning Berlin, he moved via Trebbin and Beelitz, crossing the Elbe at Wittenberg on 7 March before setting up his headquarters in Leipzig on 9 March. Gérard fell back from Frankfort an der Oder to Jüterbog, with Rechberg retreating from Kalau to Meissen, while Reynier marched to Dresden. Morand fell back from Swedish Pomerania towards Hamburg only to find that its commander had left the city fearing an uprising by the inhabitants. Tettenborn's Cossacks entered the city on 18 March to the joy of its residents. Three successive defence lines had now fallen to the Russians and Napoleon's hold on Germany was seriously threatened.

With 36,500 men and 98 guns, Eugène had bought enough time for further French formations to assemble. Added to his resources now were Lauriston's V Corps with 30,000 men and 34 guns, 1st Division (Philippon) of I Corps with 11,000 men and 16 guns, 1st Division (Dubreton) of II Corps with 8,500 men, Latour-Maubourg's 1st Cavalry Corps with 1,300 sabres and Sébastiani's 2nd Cavalry Corps with a further 1,800 sabres.

Eugène now had about 90,000 men and 148 guns at his disposal. He also had the garrisons of Madgeburg (8,000 men) and Wittenberg (5,000 men) available. The loyalties of the Saxon garrison of Torgau under General von Thielemann remained uncertain. Eugène did not have sufficient men to cover the entire line of the Elbe. However, Hamburg, at the mouth of the Elbe and part of metropolitan France, could not be abandoned and the restless Saxons, further down the Elbe, could not be left to their own devices. The Viceroy placed Marshal Davoût, commander of I Corps, in and around Dresden with 19,000 men and 60 guns. These included one brigade from Philippon's Division, the remains of Reynier's VI Corps and Gérard's Division from XI Corps. On 19 March, Davoût blew out part of the bridge across the Elbe. Eugène himself with the remainder of XI Corps and the 1st Cavalry Corps (19,000 men and 22 guns) would cover from Dresden and Torgau to the Saale River. From Philippon's Division 6,700 men and 16 guns and a further 8,000 men from Dubreton's Division held Wittenberg and Kemberg, while V Corps and 2nd Cavalry Corps (33,000 men and 42 guns) constituting the left wing, covered the area around Madgeburg from the Saale to the Havel. Eugène had only 6,000 men on the Lower Elbe under Morand and Carra St. Cyr. The remainder had deserted. His Grand Headquarters would be in Leipzig, with the 4,000 men and 8 guns of Roguet's Guards Division.

French lancer. Due to the heavy losses of both manpower and horsepower in Russia in 1812, the numbers of cavalrymen available to Napoleon was much too low for his purposes. Lacking sufficient cavalry, he was able to win battles but was not able to destroy his enemy's forces on the retreat with a vigorous pursuit.

The Treaty of Kalisch was signed on 28 February, but the delay in reaching this agreement had cost the Allies precious time and they now needed to regain the initiative. The Prussian General von Scharnhorst pleaded in favour of a rapid advance against Eugène with all available forces, but failed to win over the Russians. Prince Kutusov saw the objectives of the Russian Army achieved with the expulsion of the invader from Russian soil. More precious time was lost as the Allies debated a course of action. Finally, it was agreed that the troops in the northern theatre including the 27,000 Prussians and 120 guns under Yorck, Bülow and Borstell should be placed under Wittgenstein's command. In the southern theatre, 27,600 Prussians with 84 guns were placed under the commander of General der Kavallerie von Blücher, as was the 13,000-man-strong Russian corps under Wintzingerode. The Main Army consisted of the 33,000 men of two Russian corps under Tormassov and Miloradovich. All of these forces were to be commanded by Prince Kutusov. The plan was for Wittgenstein to move from Driesen to Berlin, to arrive there around 10 March, while Blücher would move on Dresden with the Main Army following him at a distance of three days' march. The raiding parties from Wittgenstein's Corps, consisting of about 5,000 sabres, were to operate on the Lower Elbe, while a small Prussian detachment under Tauentzien besieged Stettin and another under General von Schuler invested Glogau. A detachment of Russians under Vorontzov was to blockade Küstrin. The main axis of advance would thus be along the Upper Elbe. It was hoped that by conquering Saxony the Allies would be able to persuade Bavaria to quit its alliance with France.

Wittgenstein entered Berlin on 11 March and set about besieging Spandau. On 17 March as Cossacks clashed with the garrison of Dresden and Blücher's men advanced from Silesia, the King of Prussia founded the Landwehr (militia). Meanwhile, Sacken's Corps invested the fortress of Czestochowa garrisoned by Poniatowski's 12,000 men. It fell on 7 April and Poniatowski retired to Cracow, where he was disarmed and allowed to take his men to Saxony. Sacken's men could now join the main field army.

Napoleon's Orders to Eugène

Reacting to events, Napoleon ordered Eugène to concentrate his forces, now about 82,000 infantry, and 5,000 cavalry with 148 guns, on the Lower Elbe and take the offensive. The fall of Hamburg had been the signal for similar popular uprisings in Lüneburg, Harburg, Buxtehude and Stade. This area had been incorporated into France and constituted the 32nd Military Division, so its loss was unacceptable. Napoleon ordered Général Vandamme to move his men from Wesel on the Rhine to Bremen, from where, supported by Morand and Carra St. Cyr, he quelled the uprisings and beat off the Russian raiding-parties.

Foot artillery and train of the Imperial Guard. Famed for their heavy 12-pdrs, Napoleon's Guard Artillery often formed the core of the grand batteries that were characteristic of a number of his battles. Lacking trained infantrymen in 1813, Napoleon came to rely more on his artillery to beat his enemy. (Bellangé)

On 28 March, Napoleon placed Davoût in command of this sector of the front, held by parts of I and II Corps. Davoût moved to Lüneburg, which Dörnberg and Czernichev were using as a base for their partisan operations. The partisan leaders avoided a battle with Davoût but continued their operations. On 21 April, overall command of the Allied operations in this theatre was given to General Count Wallmoden. His forces numbered 10,000 men. By 27 April, the French had assembled a force of 40,000 men to move on Hamburg; an indication of the effectiveness of the Allied operations here and the extent of the popular uprising.

Meanwhile, Eugène moved his headquarters from Leipzig northwards to Madgeburg, joining Lauriston and Sébastiani. More of the French Army moved here to join him. By the end of March, V Corps (4 divisions, 30,500 men with 66 guns) was covering the Elbe from Kalbe to Stendal while Sébastiani's Cavalry Corps (2,000 sabres plus 400 to 500 mounted Gendarmes) was deployed above and below Madgeburg. Part of Division Philippon of II Corps (6,700 men, 8 guns) came up from the fortress of Erfurt while Roguet's Guards Division was sent from Leipzig (3,200 men with 14 guns) and Latour-Maubourg's Cavalry Corps came up from Wittenberg (2,500 sabres with 6 guns). Some of Davoût's men (Brigade Pouchelon of I Corps – 4,300 men, and Gérard's Division – 6,200 men with 16 guns) arrived from Dresden. Later, once relieved by Victor, XI Corps (18,000 men with 30 guns) joined him.

After careful preparations, Eugène moved three divisions of Lauriston's Corps across the Elbe towards Möckern on 23 March, but rumours of Allied plans to advance towards Hanover via Havelberg caused him to retrace his steps on 26 March. However, by the beginning of April, Eugène had sufficient men available to oppose any advance from Berlin by Wittgenstein; something he was to attempt a few days later at Möckern.

Wittgenstein Leaves Berlin

Wittgenstein had been in Berlin since 11 March and Yorck had arrived there on 17 March. Borstell joined them shortly afterwards. Bülow waited at Stettin until Tauentzien assembled his reserve and garrison battalions before moving on to Berlin, where he arrived on 31 March. Blücher's forces, on the Allied left, moved on Dresden. Kutusov remained in Kalisch in Silesia.

On 20 March, a council of war in Kalisch agreed that it was no longer possible to destroy Eugène's forces before Napoleon arrived. It was therefore decided to unite Wittgenstein's and Blücher's forces and hold a position along a line from Leipzig to Altenburg where they would await Napoleon's advance. Eugène was to be watched and a confrontation avoided until the union of Wittgenstein and Blücher was completed. Yorck's Corps was to move to Meissen. Bülow, supported by Borstell, was to cover the line from Madgeburg to Wittenberg. Blücher and Wintzingerode were to cross the Elbe at Dresden. The partisan warfare on the Lower Elbe would continue and the uprising in Hamburg would be supported.

As Kutusov remained in Kalisch until 7 April, when the King of Prussia persuaded him to move, Blücher at first lacked support. Wittgenstein received his orders on 24 March. Deducting the raiding-parties under Czernichev, Dörnberg and Benckendorf and the corps under Helfreich observing Spandau, he had 27,000 men, 3,500 Cossacks and 152 guns available. This force was divided into three corps under Berg (Russian), Yorck and Borstell (Prussians). Eugène's movements caused Wittgenstein to hesitate, and he awaited the arrival of Bülow's 7,000 men and 26 guns on 26 March before moving off. Hearing that Blucher's march to Altenburg was unopposed, Wittgenstein made directly for Wittenberg. By the end of March Kleist, formerly Yorck's vanguard, was at Marzahna with 5,400 men, 400 Cossacks and 26 guns. Yorck himself was at Belzig with 9,000 men and 44 guns and Berg at Brück with 8,000 men, 250 Cossacks and 62 guns. Bülow, having detached Thümen's Brigade to cover Spandau, was at Nedlitz, directly east of Madgeburg, with 3,800 men, 650 Cossacks and 12 guns.

On 31 March, after a disagreement with Scharnhorst, who favoured adopting a more defensive approach, Wittgenstein decided move on Hanover via Brunswick and to fight Eugène if he should stand at Madgeburg. He would first cross the Elbe at Rosslau and unite with Blücher in the direction of Leipzig. On 2 April, Yorck

Horse artilleryman of the Imperial Guard. The gunners of the horse artillery were normally all mounted, allowing this arm to accompany the cavalry, giving it close-range artillery support. (Bellangé)

moved on Senst, Berg on Belzig, and Kleist was ordered to take Wittenberg should Eugène abandon it.

Before these actions could be executed, Eugène crossed the Elbe at Napoleon's urging, taking 50,000 men – Roguet's Guards, V and XI Corps and Latour-Maubourg's cavalry – and 116 guns with him. Assembling at Madgeburg-Neustadt on 1 April, Eugène moved the next day with V Corps advancing against Borstell's vanguard at Königsborn, pushing it back to Nedlitz. The next day, XI Corps and Latour-Maubourg crossed the Elbe, forcing Borstell's main body back from Möckern. Bülow was in the town of Brandenburg on 3 April and force-marched his men to aid Borstell. Receiving Borstell's reports, on 2 April Wittgenstein also decided to march to support him, assembling his forces at Senst and Belzig the next day. Believing Eugène intended to march on Berlin, he ordered Borstell and Bülow to withdraw slowly on Görzke and Ziesar while he attacked the French flank. Receiving his orders during the night of 3/4 April, Borstell withdrew from Möckern in the morning, halting at Gloina and Gross-Lübars.

Eugène halted at Möckern, Gommern and Dannigkow, missing the opportunity to crush Borstell. Wittgenstein reached Zerbst on the evening of 4 April and planned to attack the French the next day, although he estimated Eugène to have 40,000 men. With only 23,000 men, 500 Cossacks and 130 guns himself, he delayed his assault to 6 April, using Borstell and Bülow to keep Eugéne's attention. He then planned to use these same forces to pin Eugène on the road from Möckern while Berg and Yorck drove into his right flank. Wittgenstein received a report, false as events proved, that Eugène was withdrawing and decided to attack immediately.

The Battle of Möckern, 5 April 1813

Wittgenstein thus found himself muddling his way into a battle before having fully concentrated his forces. Eugène enjoyed the benefit of fighting from a central position against forces disadvantaged by being spread out over a relatively large area

On Eugène's right flank Division Lagrange of V Corps (9,500 men, 16 guns) was at Wahliz with their vanguard and the 1st Light Cavalry Division at Gommern and Dannigkow. His main body consisted of the 24,000 men and 46 guns of XI Corps in three divisions at Karith, Nedlitz and Büden. The 3rd Light Cavalry Division was at Zeddenick with 800 horses and 6 guns. 1st Cavalry Corps was deployed to the front of Eugène's right and centre covering the Ehle River, which ran through marshy terrain difficult for an attacker to cross. His left flank was held by Maison's Division, also of V Corps. This consisted of 5,000 men and 18 guns at Woltersdorf. In reserve behind XI Corps he had Rochambeau's Division of 8,000 men and 16 guns. In addition Roguet's Guards Division (3,200 men, 14 guns) was at Pechau holding the Klus causeway, an important road through the marshes around Madgeburg.

Hünerbein, in command of Yorck's vangaurd, advanced towards Dannigkow, making contact with the French at noon when Lagrange's vanguard fell back to Dannigkow. Meanwhile, a small Prussian detachment moved via Dornburg towards Gommern, but reinforced by troops moving up from Gommern, the French managed to hold on until Hünerbein's men eventually took the village at bayonet-point.

Yorck's main body, accompanied by Wittgenstein, reached Leitzkau by 4.00p.m. On hearing the sounds of cannon-fire, he rushed forward to support Hünerbein. Some of the artillery saw action, but the French prevented the Prussians from making any significant advances.

Berg's vanguard, commanded by Roth, also came into action at 4.00p.m. on Yorck's right at Vehlitz. The marshy terrain restricted the movement of the two Prussian columns and the Allied assault did not begin until 6.00p.m. when Borstell's infantry arrived, having marched from Gloina. The three columns now launched a successful attack. Despite heavy losses the Italians of Brigade Zucchi of XI Corps held on until nightfall, although the provisional corps commander, Général Grenier, was severely wounded. With night falling the Allies did not pursue.

Oppen, commanding Bülow's vanguard, having the furthest to march, reached the area of Möckern about 4.00p.m. While Bülow's infantry and artillery occupied Zeddenick, Oppen's cavalry drove back the 1st Light Cavalry Division to Vehlitz, where Borstell's men finished them off. The French troops at Nedlitz fell back as well. After dark Bülow retired to Zeddenick.

Although Eugène had the advantage of internal lines of communication and superior numbers, the Allies had proved victorious. Their losses amounted to 500 men with the French losing around 2,200 men and one gun. However, the marshy terrain had restricted Eugène's movements as much as his opponents' and his men had acquitted themselves well. The Allied success can be put down in part to luck – had Wittgenstein not been misinformed about Eugène's intentions,

TOP **Général Jacques-Alexandre-Bernard Law Lauriston, (1768-1824). Son of a French general and a graduate of the École Militaire in Paris, Lauriston rose through the ranks during the Revolutionary Wars, being made a general in 1805. A veteran of several campaigns, Lauriston was a highly experienced and most capable divisional commander.**

ABOVE **Marshal Auguste-Frédéric-Louis Viesse de Marmont, Duke of Ragusa, (1774-1852). The twenty-third of Napoleon's marshals to be appointed, Marmont suffered a defeat at the hands of the Duke of Wellington at Salamanca in July 1812. Severely wounded there, he returned to France to recover before being recalled by Napoleon to participate in the campaigns of 1813 in Germany. Commanding VI Corps under the Emperor's watchful eye, Marmont performed well.**

Marshal Étienne-Jacques-Joseph Alexandre Macdonald, Duke of Tarentum (1765-1840). Awarded his marshal's baton for his performance at the Battle of Wagram in 1809, Macdonald commanded a corps in the Russian campaign of 1812 and the German Campaigns of 1813.

then he may well not have attacked – and partly to the bold decision to attack a superior force. That night, Eugène fell back to Madgeburg, crossing to the west bank of the Elbe the next day. All the river crossings were destroyed, as was the Klus causeway, and Eugène abandoned any thoughts of an advance on Berlin. The first battle of the campaign had been an Allied victory – there were firm hopes this presaged greater success.

The Allies cross the Elbe

As Eugène had apparently abandoned any intentions of advancing on Berlin, Wittgenstein began preparations to cross the Elbe himself. Wittenberg was now cut off with a screen of Cossacks to its west and invested by Kleist, while Bülow and Borstell took up positions around Madgeburg. These siege operations reduced the forces available to Wittgenstein – with reinforcements, Berg and Yorck together now numbered 18,000 men, 700 Cossacks and 92 guns. Furthermore, the Elbe crossing at Rosslau was precariously situated between two French-occupied fortresses at Madgeburg and Wittenberg, which limited its usefulness. Wittgenstein decided to await reinforcements before making his next major move. On 17 April he did try to take Wittenberg by surprise, but his assault columns were driven off. This fortress was then left under observation by a small force under the Russian General von Harpe.

On 23 April, Voronzow's Corps replaced Bülow, arriving from Küstrin where it was replaced by Kapzevitch's Division. On 25 April, Bülow's 4,800 men, 400 Cossacks and 20 guns reached Dessau. Once there he was ordered to cover the bridgehead at Rosslau and place outposts in Aken and Köthen. Kleist now moved forwards marching to Halle while Helfreich joined Berg at Landsberg. Wittgenstein now had 22,000 men, 2,250 Cossacks and 143 guns. Spandau capitulated on 24 April, allowing the 3,000 men of Thümen's command to join them. By the end of April Wittgenstein had his headquarters in Leipzig along with Berg's Corps. Yorck, Kleist and Bülow were all nearby at Schkeuditz, Halle and Köthen respectively.

Meanwhile, Eugène had completed his withdrawal across the Elbe. News arrived of Morand's defeat at Hamburg at around the same time as the bridgehead at Rosslau was established. Eugène now feared being shut up in Madgeburg and cut off from his lines of communication to the fortress of Wesel on the Rhine and the River Main to the south. He wheeled south and took up a new position, securing his flanks on the Harz Mountains and Elbe. From there, Eugène would be able to concentrate his army quickly and threatened the right flank of the Allies while leaving himself the option of a further withdrawal. He reinforced the garrison of Madgeburg with parts of the Divisions of Philippon and Dubreton, bringing it up to about 10,000 men. The remainder of Philippon's Division took up positions to the north of the city, while Victor covered its south along the lower Saale with the rest of Dubreton's Division and some cavalry. Eugène positioned Roguet's Guards Division,

V and XI Corps (Gérard replaced the wounded provisional commander Grenier, pending Macdonald's arrival) and Latour-Maubourg's Cavalry Corps – 50,000 men and 141 guns – roughly along the line of the Wipper River, facing south.

Blücher's Movements

By mid-March, Blücher's raiding parties had crossed the Elbe both above and below Dresden and his vanguard, Wintzingerode's Corps, reached Bautzen on 20 March. Meanwhile, Durutte had completed his withdrawal from Dresden, so that when Wintzingerode entered the Saxon capital on 27 March he found it abandoned by the French. He erected a pontoon bridge and continued his advance, reaching Leipzig by 3 April. His raiding parties crossed the Saale at various points on 8 April and Lanskoi covered them by occupying Merseburg.

Blücher himslef advanced from Breslau (Wroclaw) in Silesia on 16 March and was in Dresden by the end of the month. Fearing a French move from the direction of Erfurt or Hof, he moved south towards Chemnitz. By 4 April, he had reached the upper Mulde at Zwickau and Penig, where he remained for the time being. As Saxony had not joined the Allies and her king had departed for Regensburg, leaving his government in the hands of commissioners, his domain was treated as enemy territory. Despite calls to join the Allied cause, the populace as a whole showed little enthusiasm.

The general indecision in the Allied high command again led to inactivity. Blücher's three Prussian brigades took up positions in Penig, Zwickau and Nossen, the Reserve Cavalry at Kohren. Scouting parties were sent out to observe French movements and to link up with Wintzingerode's partisans with patrols spreading throughout the province of Thuringia.

Napoleon arrives in Germany

These patrols brought back unpleasant news. Napoleon was said to have arrived in Thuringia, concentrating his main army around Erfurt and moving to join Eugène. The Allies reacted by drawing their forces together. Wintzingerode was ordered close up on Blücher. By the evening of 25 April, he was approaching Borna, with his cavalry at Merseburg, Lützen and Weissenfels. Blücher had concentrated his forces at Borna, Altenburg and Mittweida.

At last, the main Allied army began to advance, albeit at a snail's pace. Miloradovich's Corps had left Glogau in Silesia on 9 April, but did not reach Dresden until 22 April, from where it was ordered to Chemnitz, where it arrived on 26 April. Tormassov's Corps, which had left Kalisch on 6 April, reaching Dresden on the 24th. One of its divisions, that under Prince Gorchakov, was sent on to Meissen. By the time Napoleon was ready to cross the Saale, the Allies had assembled about 100,000 men. Bülow was at Dessau with 5,000 men, 400 Cossacks and 20 guns. Wittgenstein had a further 22,000 men with 2,200 Cossacks and 143 guns around Halle, Zörbig and Landsberg. The 37,000 men of Blücher's command along with 3,500 Cossacks and 156 guns were deployed in a line Leipzig–Borna–Altenburg and at Mittweida. The main Allied filed army was deployed around Dresden and Chemnitz with 29,000 men, 3,000 Cossacks and 266 guns.

Marshal Nicolas-Charles Oudinot, Duke of Reggio (1767-1847). Appointed to the rank of marshal in 1809, Oudinot was twice wounded in Russia in 1812. He recovered sufficiently to command a corps again in 1813.

Josef Anton, Prince Poniatowski, (1763-1813). A Polish patriot and member of the royal house, Poniatowski's forces were unable to participate in the Spring Campaign of 1813.

Russian Jäger. Supposedly a light infantry formation, by this stage of the Napoleonic Wars the distinction between line and light troops had become blurred. Nevertheless, Russian Jäger were considered to be a crack force. (Richard Knötel)

Napoleon left St. Cloud to join his army on the night of 15/16 April. Two days later, he reached Mainz, where he met Berthier at Headquarters with the Imperial Guard. Events had forced the Emperor to leave Paris earlier than he had intended. Eugène's retreat across the Saale, the crossing of the Elbe by the Allies, the uprising in Hamburg, concerns about the actions of Austria and Saxony, the Prussian re-armament and the approach of Russian reinforcements forced Napoleon to react. He did so with fewer forces to hand than he had hoped.

Napoleon spent the next two weeks doing his best to accelerate the mobilisation of his forces. He lacked everything, particularly officers, artillery pieces and horses. However, by the end of April, he had assembled 228,000 men and 460 guns. Taking away the 48,000 men and 140 guns under Eugène's command, Napoleon had the Imperial Guard, the Corps of Ney, Bertrand, Marmont and Oudinot, and the Cavalry Corps of Latour-Maubourg at his disposal. They amounted to 130,000 men with 320 guns. Eugène's forces were designated the 'Army of the Elbe', while Napoleon's was known as the 'Army of the Main'. The Emperor intended to link his forces with those of Eugène and he marched from south-west Germany on Naumburg. The hilly terrain of

Frederick August, King of Saxony. Forced into an unwilling alliance with Prussia in 1806, Frederick August soon became an ally of Napoleon, receiving his royal crown as a reward. He sat on the fence at the beginning of 1813 before deciding for Napoleon. Napoleon's defeat at Leipzig would cost him half his kingdom.

Viceroy Eugène de Beauharnais (1781-1824). Son of Josephine, Napoleon's first wife, Eugène was left holding Germany while Napoleon assembled a new army. He conducted this difficult task with some skill, being forced to abandon Berlin but holding the line of the River Elbe.

Thuringia would help limit the effect of the Allies' superiority in cavalry. From here he could also move on Leipzig and thus threaten both Berlin and Dresden. He could expect Berlin, the Prussian capital, to be defended and Dresden was on the Russian line of retreat to Silesia. By threatening both cities he hoped to force the Allies to divide their forces. He also hoped that by operating close to the Austrian border and in Saxony, he could bring these waverers over to his side.

For the advance Ney's Corps, the vanguard, was allocated the road running from Würzburg via Meiningen, Erfurt and Weimar to Naumburg. The Guard and Marmont were to march from Hanau via Fulda to Eisenach, before following Ney. Bertrand's Corps, on its way from Italy, was to march via Bamberg and Koburg to Saalfeld.

When Napoleon arrived in Erfurt on 25 April to take command of his army, the leading elements of Ney's Corps were in a line running from Auerstadt via Dornburg to Jena. The vanguard of the Imperial Guard was at Weimar with its main body in Erfurt. Bertrand was between Saalfeld and Sonneberg, his division of Württembergers under Franquemont at Hildburghausen. In Napoleon's second line was Marmont around Eisenach and Langensalza. Oudinot's newly formed Corps with the Divisions of Pacthod and Lorencez (transferred from Bertrand's Corps) was at Bamberg and Nuremberg (Nürnberg), and Raglovich's Bavarian Division at Bayreuth and Müncheberg.

Eugène was ordered to move towards the Saale, closing up on Ney's left and holding the crossings at Wettin, Halle and Merseburg. However, by 25 April only Division Fressinet had moved. Napoleon had not achieved his objective of reaching the line of the Saale by 25 April. On arriving at Erfurt he found his forces ill-prepared to take the offensive and spent the next four days doing what he could to alleviate their problems.

By the evening of 30 April Napoleon's forces had closed up to the Saale with Ney's forces beyond Weissenfels. Eugène was to the north around Halle and Merseburg. A number of minor actions had been fought including one at Wettin on the Saale on 27 April where the Prussians withdrew without loss after blowing up the bridge. The next day at Halle Lauriston fought Kleist for several hours before the French withdrew. Once Merseburg and Weissenfels had fallen, the Prussians evacuated Halle. Napoleon's offensive had started well and the performance of his 'Marie-Louises' pleased him particularly. He had now linked up with Eugène. Napoleon pressed on, hoping to catch the Allies before they had fully assembled their forces and crush them.

Russian line infantry. It was the Russian line infantry that formed the backbone of the Allied war effort at the beginning of 1813. Having suffered almost as much as Napoleon's forces, the weakened battalions that marched into Germany at the beginning of 1813 were hardy veterans indeed. (Richard Knötel)

1. Eugène's Army of the Elbe advances to secure the crossings of the Saale.
2. 29 April – Macdonald (who had replaced St.Cyr) fights an action at Merseburg.
3. 28 April – Lauriston is repulsed by Kleist at Halle.
4. 29 April – Souham's Division (from Ney's Corps) drives the Russian force from Weissenfels.
5. Night of 30 April – With the French across the Saale at Merseburg and Weissenfels, Kleist retires from Halle.
6. Napoleon's Army of the Main advances.
7. 8,000-man French garrison of Magdeburg closely watched by detachments of Bülow's Corps.
8. 5,000-man French garrison of Wittenberg besieged by detachments of Bülow's Corps.
9. French garrison of 3,000 besieged in Spandau, capitulates on 24 April.
10. French garrison of 5,000 besieged.
11. French garrison of 5,000 besieged.
12. Saxon garrison of Torgau (General Thielemann) declares neutrality, refusing to let either side use the bridge over the Elbe.
13. Allied troops advance to support Blücher and Wittgenstein. Tormassov reaches Dresden on 24 April.

The Allied Countermoves

When Kutusov took to his deathbed on 18 April, a power vacuum was left in the Allied supreme command. Napoleon's arrival in Germany made it clear that the Allies now had two choices; either to be pushed back by a French advance or to go over to the offensive themselves against a numerically stronger enemy, but one that lacked sufficient cavalry and whose infantry was of comparatively poor quality. It was decided to attack and the Allied forces began to concentrate around Altenburg with the aim of attacking the French right flank.

On Kutusov's death on 28 April, Wittgenstein was appointed his successor. At 44 years old, he was a relatively young man for his position and reacted quickly. He was perceptive enough to appreciate that Napoleon's initial objective was the line of the Elbe, so he decided to strike before Napoleon got there. This strategy was risky for if he were defeated Napoleon would be in a position to cut his line of retreat through Dresden. Communications with Silesia would be cut and the Allies would be driven away from Austria and a potential ally. Nevertheless the plan was to attack the French flank as they marched towards Leipzig on 2 May. Between 26 and 30 April Wittgenstein's forces concentrated around Zwenkau with Blücher at Borna. By the evening of 30 April the French army and that of the Allies were so close to each other that a battle was inevitable.

Russian dragoons. The Allies enjoyed superiority in both the number and quality of their cavalry. The Russian dragoons were standard battle cavalry. (Richard Knötel)

Napoleon's Moves

Lacking sufficient cavalry, the information Napoleon had on the evening of 30 April about Allied movements was sparse. He expected the Allied headquarters to display little energy and to be able to defeat Wittgenstein at Altenburg before moving on Blücher's rear. His orders for 1 May indicate that he was expecting a battle that day. Ney was to move on a wide front on Lützen. Marmont was to get as close as possible to Weissenfels to support Ney if required. Eugène was to move via Merseburg towards Schladebach and if he heard gunfire coming from Lützen to move against the Allies' flank.

At 9.00a.m., Ney's Corps started moving and around 11.00a.m. his vanguard reached the village of Rippach, where it clashed with Wintzingerode's forward units under Lanskoi. The French pushed them back easily, but during the action a cannonball fatally injured the commander of the Guard Cavalry, Marshal Bessières. That afternoon, the artillery of both Corps engaged each other between Röcken and Starsiedel, the duel ending with the Allies withdrawing behind the Flossgraben. Ney followed up as far as the village of Kaja, where he established his headquarters. While his vanguard and Souham's Division bivouacked between the villages of Kaja, Rahna, Grossgörschen and

Kleingörschen, his other divisions spent the night at Starsiedel, Kaja and Lützen. While Marchand's Division covered the crossing of the Flossgraben on the road from Lützen to Leipzig, the divisions of Compans and Bonet from Marmont's Corps came up behind Ney, along the road from Weissenfels to Rippach. Friedrich's Division was still at Naumburg, about 13 km from Weissenfels.

During the course of the day, Bertrand's Corps moved up to the area around Jena, while Oudinot's Corps reached Kahla. Roguet's Division, now detached from Eugène, rejoined the remainder of the Imperial Guard at Weissenfels.

Eugène's Army of the Elbe marched via Rippach towards the sounds of the guns. By evening, it had linked up with Lauriston and Latour-Maubourg in the area of Markranstädt. Durutte's Division, now 4,000 men strong thanks to the transfer of five battalions from Marmont's Corps, reached Merseburg. Napoleon now had 144,000 men and 372 guns within striking distance of his enemies, but of this formidable force only 7,500 were cavalry.

Should a battle take place, Wittgenstein was in a position to call on 88,500 men (19,000 of which were cavalry), 5,000 Cossacks and 552 guns. However, faults in the Allied command structure were going to make it difficult for him to do so. For the proposed Allied flank attack to succeed they would need to move swiftly and decisively and the attacks would need to be co-ordinated. Under any circumstances this level of organisation was a daunting task. With a multinational force that had not fought together before and in which certain commanders were, for their own reasons, being less than fully co-operative it would be doubly difficult.

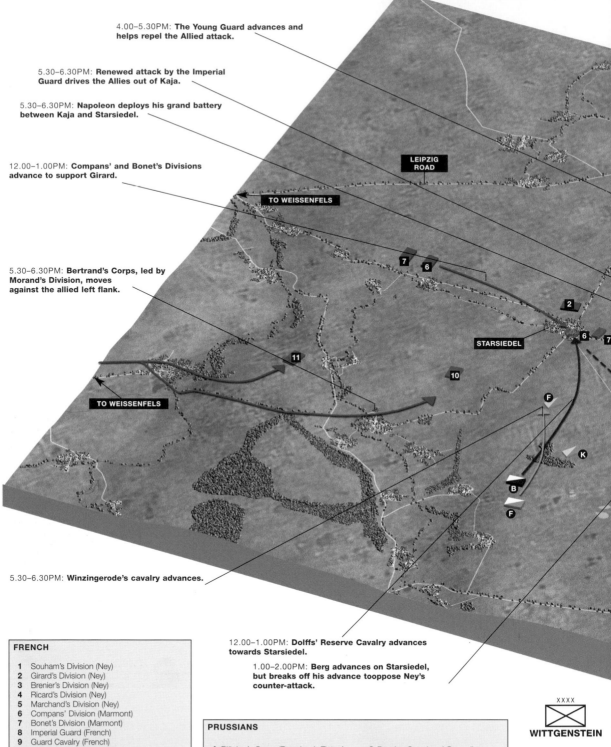

4.00–5.30PM: The Young Guard advances and helps repel the Allied attack.

5.30–6.30PM: Renewed attack by the Imperial Guard drives the Allies out of Kaja.

5.30–6.30PM: Napoleon deploys his grand battery between Kaja and Starsiedel.

12.00–1.00PM: Compans' and Bonet's Divisions advance to support Girard.

5.30–6.30PM: Bertrand's Corps, led by Morand's Division, moves against the allied left flank.

5.30–6.30PM: Winzingerode's cavalry advances.

LEIPZIG ROAD

TO WEISSENFELS

STARSIEDEL

TO WEISSENFELS

12.00–1.00PM: Dolffs' Reserve Cavalry advances towards Starsiedel.

1.00–2.00PM: Berg advances on Starsiedel, but breaks off his advance tooppose Ney's counter-attack.

XXXX

WITTGENSTEIN

FRENCH

1 Souham's Division (Ney)
2 Girard's Division (Ney)
3 Brenier's Division (Ney)
4 Ricard's Division (Ney)
5 Marchand's Division (Ney)
6 Compans' Division (Marmont)
7 Bonet's Division (Marmont)
8 Imperial Guard (French)
9 Guard Cavalry (French)
10 Morand's Division (Bertrand)
11 Peyri's Division (Bertrand)
12 Macdonald's Corps (French)
13 Latour-Maubourg's Cavalry Corps (French)
14 Kellermann's Cavalry
15 Young Guard (French)
16 Old Guard (French)
17 Ney's Corps (French)
18 Grand Battery (French)
NB Solid symbols show first positions; 'ghosted' symbols show second positions.

PRUSSIANS

A Blücher's Corps (Prussians): Zieten's & Klux's Brigades in front line, Roeder's in second line
B Dolffs' Reserve Cavalry (Prussians)
C Yorck's Corps (Prussians)

RUSSIANS

D Berg's Corps (Russians)
E Eugene of Württemberg's Corps (Witzingerode) (Russians)
F Wittgenstein's Cavalry

G Russian Guard and Grenadiers
H St. Priest's Division (Eugene of Württemberg)
I 2nd Grenadier Division (Konovnizin)
J 1st Grenadier Division (Konovnizin)
K Gallitzin's Cavalry Corps
L Russian Reserve
NB Solid symbols show first positions; 'ghosted' symbols show second positions.

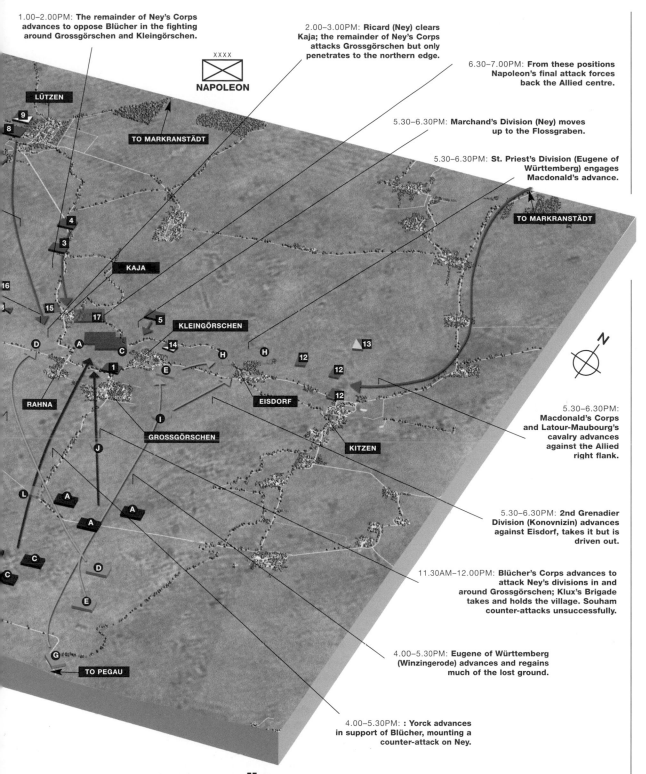

1.00–2.00PM: The remainder of Ney's Corps advances to oppose Blücher in the fighting around Grossgörschen and Kleingörschen.

2.00–3.00PM: Ricard (Ney) clears Kaja; the remainder of Ney's Corps attacks Grossgörschen but only penetrates to the northern edge.

6.30–7.00PM: From these positions Napoleon's final attack forces back the Allied centre.

5.30–6.30PM: Marchand's Division (Ney) moves up to the Flossgraben.

5.30–6.30PM: St. Priest's Division (Eugene of Württemberg) engages Macdonald's advance.

XXXX

NAPOLEON

LÜTZEN

TO MARKRANSTÄDT

TO MARKRANSTÄDT

KAJA

KLEINGÖRSCHEN

RAHNA

EISDORF

GROSSGÖRSCHEN

KITZEN

N

5.30–6.30PM: Macdonald's Corps and Latour-Maubourg's cavalry advances against the Allied right flank.

5.30–6.30PM: 2nd Grenadier Division (Konovnizin) advances against Eisdorf, takes it but is driven out.

11.30AM–12.00PM: Blücher's Corps advances to attack Ney's divisions in and around Grossgörschen; Klux's Brigade takes and holds the village. Souham counter-attacks unsuccessfully.

4.00–5.30PM: Eugene of Württemberg (Winzingerode) advances and regains much of the lost ground.

TO PEGAU

4.00–5.30PM: : Yorck advances in support of Blücher, mounting a counter-attack on Ney.

THE BATTLE OF LÜTZEN

2 May 1813, 11.30am–6.30pm, viewed from the south east showing the initial Prussian and Russian attacks around Grossgörschen and Starsiedel, the French counterattacks and the flanking movements of Bertrand's and Macdonald's Corps.

THE BATTLES

LÜTZEN, 2 MAY 1813

Wittgenstein intended to attack on the morning of 2 May between the Flossgraben and Grunabach. He ordered Wintzingerode to assemble at Werben and cover Blücher's advance, which allowed Blücher to cross the Elster at 5.00am dividing into two columns at Storkwitz and Pegau to take up his positions by 6.00am. Yorck and Berg were to follow Blücher closely, while Miloradovich was to cover their left flank at Zeitz. Kleist was ordered to draw the attention of any French troops moving on Leipzig, but if outnumbered to fall back on Wurzen.

Things started to go wrong for the Allies almost immediately. The crossing at Zwenkau was considered insecure as Wintzingerode had unexpectedly fallen back to Schkorlopp. Thus, instead of being ordered to cross the Elster and Flossgraben on a broad front, Blücher, Yorck and Berg were all ordered across the Elster at Pegau, causing a bottleneck and delays. In addition with Miloradovich so far back at Zeitz he could not effectively cover the Allied left and Bertrand was able to move against it.

Wintzingerode marched to Werben via Gross-Schkorlopp and Klein-Schkorlopp, reaching there by 6.00am. Blücher, whose Corps was supposed to form the front line, marched off from Rötha late on 1 May, reaching Audigast by 5.00am, but his line of marched crossed those of Yorck and Berg, causing delays. The Main Army followed Blücher to Groitzsch, arriving there on time but then waiting for hours until the confusion in the supporting columns had been overcome. Only then could it march to Stönzsch. Once the Allied columns had crossed the Elster and Flossgraben, they moved to the left, a low ridge hiding this movement from the French, and the Allies were able to draw up in a line from Werben to Domsen facing Starsiedel. It was only now the Allies noticed that the French held the villages of Gross and Kleingörschen, Kaja and Rahna, so a move to the right was ordered. By 11.00am the Allied army was drawn up with the first line consisting of Blücher's Corps with Zieten and Klüx's Brigades in front and Roeder in support and the Reserve Cavalry under Dolffs 2 km to the left. The second line consisted of Berg's Corps on the right flank and Yorck's on the left. The third line consisted of Wintzingerode's infantry under Duke Eugene of Württemberg, with his cavalry on the left flank towards Domsen. The Main Army was supposed to form up behind the rear centre, but having been delayed, did not take up its positions until just before 4.00pm.

In Blücher's and Yorck's Corps (34 battalions of infantry, 51 squadrons of cavalry and 132 guns) the Prussians had 33,000 men. Berg's and Wintzingerode's Russian Corps and Main Army fielded another 60 battalions of infantry, 85 squadrons of cavalry and 275 guns,

– 34,000 men in all. This gave the Allied army a combined battlefield strength of 67,000 men with, additionally, 2,300 Cossacks.

Napoleon's Orders

On the evening of 1 May, Napoleon was unsure of the positions and intentions of the Allies. All he could do was order his men to close up on each other to be ready for any eventuality. He ordered Mortier with the Imperial Guard to move from Weissenfels to Lützen. Marmont, who had two divisions at Rippach, was ordered to bring up the third from Naumburg, while Bertrand, less Franquemont's Württembergers, was ordered to Starsiedel. Oudinot was to continue to Naumburg and Ney and Eugène received orders to hold the positions occupied that evening.

The information received during the night of 1/2 May was too thin to make any major decisions. Ney's report that Wintzingerode was moving from Zwenkau to Pegau was correct and Eugène reported that there was only a small Allied force in Leipzig and that the troops there earlier had moved to an unknown destination. Rumours coming from Leipzig reported that the Allied headquarters had moved to Rochlitz on 30 April. This suggested to Napoleon that the Allies were concentrating south of Leipzig. He considered attempting to envelope them there, but it was not clear if they were taking up defensive positions or preparing to attack Napoleon's right flank. He decided to continue moving his left on Leipzig, to have his centre stand facing the Elster and to close his right up on it. If the Allies failed to move on 2 May, this would leave him the opportunity to attack them on 3 May frontally along the Elster with his centre and right while his left moved via Leipzig to envelope them. If, however, the Allies did attack on 2 May, his centre, Ney's Corps of five divisions, could hold their positions while his left and right moved against the Allied flanks.

On the morning of 2 May, Napoleon ordered Lauriston to Leipzig, Macdonald to Markranstädt and Ney to remain in his positions. All three corps commanders were to send strong reconnaissance to Leipzig, Pegau and Zwenkau as well as keeping in close contact with each other. Bertrand was to reach Kaja with two divisions by 3.00am, while Marmont was to assemble his three divisions at Rippach.

French Movements

Lauriston moved at 9.00am towards Leipzig while Macdonald joined the 1st Cavalry Corps at Markranstädt. Bertrand departed Stössen at 6.00am,

Cossacks. These irregular cavalry formations were a common element of the Russian Army in this period. While their performance on the battlefield was not as disciplined as that of their regular counterparts, they were effective raiders and skirmishers. (Richard Knötel)

marching off in the direction of Starsiedel, but he halted on the heights of Dippelsdorf on receiving reports of an Allied corps at Zeitz – this was Miloradovich. The Guard reached Lützen, while Marmont's three divisions concentrated at Rippach. Ney, however, neither concentrated his divisions nor sent out any patrols. Being apparently unaware of Napoleon's intentions, he did not want to exhaust his Marie-Louises unnecessarily. As a result of this oversight Napoleon received no reports of the Allied movement across the Elster at Pegau and a few hours later the Allies were to give Ney a nasty surprise.

For Napoleon the morning passed without the fog of war clearing. At 8.00am, he ordered XI Corps to a position halfway between Markranstädt and Leipzig. This left him the option of supporting Lauriston at Leipzig or moving towards Zwenkau. At 9.00am, having heard nothing from Ney to the contrary, Napoleon assumed the Allies were adopting a defensive posture and issued orders for Bertrand's leading division to move to Taucha that day, Marmont to move to Pegau before dark, and Ney, should Marmont make contact with the Allies, to move in support. The Guard and headquarters were to remain in Lützen. Napoleon was intending to occupy the Allies frontally while moving around their right at Leipzig.

When Bertrand moved from Dippelsdorf to Granschütz strong detachments of Cossacks brought him to a halt. Ney still did nothing, while Marmont moved off from Rippach between 10.00 and 11.00am towards Pegau. Eugène sent Gérard and the 1st Cavalry Corps to Schönau to support Lauriston if necessary, while Fressinet and Charpentier were ordered to form a front against the Elster between Markranstädt and Lausen from where they could also move on Pegau if necessary.

About 10.00am, Lauriston made contact with Kleist at Lindenau. Weight of numbers told and Kleist was forced out of Leipzig by 2.00pm. He fell back to Wurzen by that evening, followed up by Maison. Napoleon, hearing cannon-fire coming from around Grossgörschen, halted the two other divisions of V Corps on the road to Markranstädt. About the same time, Napoleon, accompanied by Ney, left his headquarters at Lützen and rode towards Lindenau to observe the action there. Suddenly, a report arrived from Pegau, followed by the sounds of heavy artillery fire coming from Kaja. He ordered Ney to return to his corps immediately, ordering him to hold his positions. He then instructed Marmont to accelerate his march to Starsiedel and join Ney's right flank. Bertrand was ordered to move to Söhesten and attack the Allied left. Meanwhile, Macdonald and the 1st Cavalry Corps were to halt and await developments. Maison was to remain in Leipzig, while Lauriston's two other divisions were to move in the direction of Zwenkau. The Guard was to remain in reserve at Lützen. In a very short time, Napoleon had put together a plan that would allow him to tie

2nd East Prussian Infantry Regiment. This plate shows the various dress worn by Prussian officers at this time. From left to right, officer in greatcoat, officer in undress, officer in full dress, fusilier (light infantry) lieutenant in field dress, grenadier lieutenant in parade dress, officer with cap and frock coat. (Richard Knötel)

down the Allies frontally, while sweeping around both their flanks and defeating them. He had a chance for the decisive victory he sought.

The Battle for Grossgörschen, Kleingörschen, Kaja and Rahna

While Napoleon was issuing his orders, a bitter and bloody battle was taking place in and around Grossgörschen. Blücher's Corps had taken a brief rest following their exhausting night march, but at around 11.30am they left the shelter of the low ridge and launched the opening attack of the Battle of Lützen. To the north in front of Blücher's Corps stood the four villages of Grossgörschen, Rahna, Kleingörschen and Kaja. They formed a rectangle about 1 km square filled with trees and bushes, marshy in places and cut by ditches. The area around the villages was relatively open.

About noon, Blücher's front line came into cannon range and the alarm sounded in the French encampment. The Allies thought Ney's men were the vanguard of a force at Lützen. Reports of a cloud of dust over the road from Weissenfels to Leipzig suggested the French Army was moving towards Leipzig and it was hoped to take their flank and possibly their rear with this attack. Rather than now rushing Ney's surprised men, time was wasted bringing up the artillery and bombarding the French encampment for 40 minutes. Only then was Klüx's Brigade sent to storm the quadrangle of villages. Souham's Division was overwhelmed and Grossgörschen fell to the first charge, after which Klüx easily beat off several local counter-attacks.

Meanwhile, the Prussian Reserve Cavalry moved towards Starsiedel. Here too, the surprised French, Girard's Division, were given a chance to assemble while the Allies methodically brought up the artillery. The divisions of Compans and Bonet from Marmont's Corps used the delay to move up to Starsiedel and deploy their artillery. The Allied attack now bogged down, the opportunity given by their surprise attack having been wasted.

Souham now counter-attacked and cleared Grossgörschen. Blücher then sent Zieten in to take Kleingörschen and by 1.00pm he had captured this village. Klüx then moved against Grossgörschen once again and retook it. Rahna too fell to the Prussians, but the divisions of Brenier and Ricard moved to counter-attack. Ney arrived on the battlefield now and threw in Souham and Girard, supported by Brenier, against Kleingörschen. They recaptured Rahna and Kleingörschen, but were unable to retake Grossgörschen, despite superior numbers.

Berg then moved up to the left to attack Starsiedel, his movement coinciding with Ney's counter-attack and the loss of Rahna and Klcingörschen to the French. As a result Berg halted to the south-west of Rahna while Blücher's last reserve, Roeder's Brigade, moved up supported by the fire of his entire artillery, 104 guns. The French fell back from Kleingörschen and Rahna and the Prussian Guard Fusilier Battalion even took Kaja. Shortly after 2.00pm Ney's entire line fell back. Losses were heavy on both sides. One determined charge by the large

1st and 2nd Silesian Infantry Regiments. This plate is also useful as it shows the various types of dress worn by Prussian infantry at this time. From left to right, fusilier NCO in summer dress, musketeer in field dress, private in fatigues, private in greatcoat, musketeer NCO in winter parade dress, musketeer NCO in field dress. (Richard Knötel)

mass of Allied cavalry may well have settled the issue, but Napoleon now arrived, greeted by cries of 'Vive l'Empereur!' The situation was worse than he thought and his centre might collapse before his flanking manoeuvre could take effect. He needed to stabilise the situation in his centre to allow enough time for the flank march to take effect. While Napoleon's aides rode off to Eugène and Bertrand to hurry them along, Ney's last reserve, Ricard, went over to the attack. They quickly cleared Kaja before moving on Grossgörschen. Supported by the rallied remnants of Ney's other divisions and a battery of artillery well positioned between Kaja and Starsiedel, they took the northern edge of that village before their attack ground to a halt.

Little progress was being made on the French right. Marmont, faced with 12,000 Russian and Prussian cavalry and Berg's Corps, had little choice but to remain largely immobile. However, his presence had enough effect for Wittgenstein to delay sending in Yorck and Berg to support Blücher, particularly as the Russian reserves had yet to reach the battlefield. The only thing Wittgenstein did was reinforce the artillery deployed against Starsiedel to about 100 guns.

1st and 2nd West Prussian Infantry Regiments. This plate shows a typical Prussian infantryman of 1813 in action. One wonders how many soldiers from an impoverished Prussia really did carry the full regulation kit. (Richard Knötel)

Just before 4.00pm the Russian Main Army finally reached height 172, later called the 'Monarchs' Hill'. This hill no longer exists, as part of the battlefield has been strip-mined. Wittgenstein then went over to the offensive again, sending in Yorck's Corps. Supported by artillery and cavalry, Hünerbein's Brigade moved on Kleingörschen, Horn's on Rahna. These fresh troops, supported by the remainder of Blücher's men, took Kleingörschen and Rahna for the third time. For a short time, the Prussians even held Kaja, but a counter-attack by a brigade of the Young Guard pushed them back. Close combat took place for about 90 minutes. Ney, Blücher and Scharnhorst were wounded; the latter succumbing to an infection from this wound some weeks later. With another wave of counter-attacks the French regained Kleingörschen and Rahna, but the respite was short-lived, and the infantry of the 2nd Russian Corps under Duke Eugene of Württemberg recaptured all four villages. The remains of Ney's Corps now fell back to the far side of Kaja.

It was now around 5.30pm and despite their apparent success the Allies had by now lost all chance of victory. French reinforcements were

arriving; Marchand's Division from Ney's Corps moved along the north bank of the Flossgraben, taking positions opposite Kleingörschen. At the same time, the leading elements of Morand's Division of Bertrand's Corps reached Kölzen. Macdonald's Corps moved from Markranstädt towards Eisdorf in battle-order. As Wittgenstein had used up most of his reserves fending off an attack from the Imperial Guard, he had insufficient men left to oppose them. Defeat was now inevitable.

Around 6.00pm another attack by the Young Guard drove the Allies out of Kaja. Meanwhile, Napoleon brought up 80 guns, deploying them along the ridge running from Kaja to Starsiedel. About the same time, Macdonald and Latour-Maubourg's cavalry reached Eisdorf. Fressinet's Division launched an assault on that village, while Charpentier's moved on Kitzen. Gérard followed up behind them. St Priest's Division of the 2nd Russian Corps was driven out of Eisdorf, but then counter-attacked, regaining the village, only to lose it again to a second French assault. The Russian 2nd Grenadier Division now moved up and retook Eisdorf. However, Gérard's counter-attack proved decisive. All the Allies could now do was prevent Eugène from crossing the Flossgraben before nightfall.

Napoleon led the final, decisive attack in the centre in person. Marchand gradually worked his way over the Flossgraben to take Kleingörschen while Bonnet's Division now moved against Rahna and Napoleon ordered 'la Garde au feu!' Supported by the remains of III Corps, four columns under Mortier descended upon Grossgörschen from Kaja. The Allies were driven back in a state of chaos, abandoning all the positions gained that day at such great cost. Darkness fell at 7.00pm and the fighting died down, although parts of the Brigades of Klüx and Zieten disputed Grossgörschen into the night.

ABOVE **Major von Lützow. In March 1813, Lützow was given permission to raise a free corps of German non-Prussians to fight in the coming war. His force came to include both infantry and cavalry and was seen as a symbol of German nationalism.**

LEFT **Lützow's recruitment office in the Gasthof zum goldenen Zepter, Breslau (Wroclaw), Silesia. This free corps attracted patriots, students, intellectuals and adventurers. Although not of great military value, its exploits have formed the stuff of myth and legend.**

Beaten and in danger of being enveloped, the Allies had no choice but to fall back. They started rallying to the south of Eisdorf, Grossgörschen and Rahna, crossing the Flossgraben under the cover of night. Duke Eugene of Württemberg and Miloradovich formed the rearguard and covered the retreat. Nine squadrons of Blücher's Reserve Cavalry clashed in the darkness with Marmont at Rahna, persuading the French not to consider a pursuit.

Losses were heavy on both sides, the French suffering about 22,000 casualties, 15,000 of which were to Ney's Corps alone. Two generals had been killed, nine severely wounded and 30 regimental commanders were *hors de combat*. The Allies captured five guns and disabled 22 others, losing two themselves. They lost suffered around 11,500 casualties including 8,500 Prussians. 53 Prussian officers died and 244 were wounded.

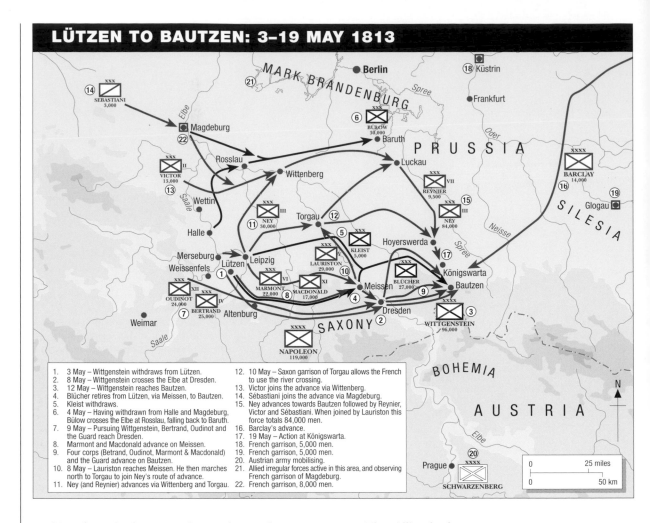

LÜTZEN TO BAUTZEN: 3–19 MAY 1813

1. 3 May – Wittgenstein withdraws from Lützen.
2. 8 May – Wittgenstein crosses the Elbe at Dresden.
3. 12 May – Wittgenstein reaches Bautzen.
4. Blücher retires from Lützen, via Meissen, to Bautzen.
5. Kleist withdraws.
6. 4 May – Having withdrawn from Halle and Magdeburg, Bülow crosses the Elbe at Rosslau, falling back to Baruth.
7. 9 May – Pursuing Wittgenstein, Bertrand, Oudinot and the Guard reach Dresden.
8. Marmont and Macdonald advance on Meissen.
9. Four corps (Betrand, Oudinot, Marmont & Macdonald) and the Guard advance on Bautzen.
10. 8 May – Lauriston reaches Meissen. He then marches north to Torgau to join Ney's route of advance.
11. Ney (and Reynier) advances via Wittenberg and Torgau.
12. 10 May – Saxon garrison of Torgau allows the French to use the river crossing.
13. Victor joins the advance via Wittenberg.
14. Sébastiani joins the advance via Magdeburg.
15. Ney advances towards Bautzen followed by Reynier, Victor and Sébastiani. When joined by Lauriston this force totals 84,000 men.
16. Barclay's advance.
17. 19 May – Action at Königswarta.
18. French garrison, 5,000 men.
19. French garrison, 5,000 men.
20. Austrian army mobilising.
21. Allied irregular forces active in this area, and observing French garrison of Magdeburg.
22. French garrison, 8,000 men.

Napoleon had won a victory, but only at great cost. The Allies had fought bravely, but thanks to the mishandling of their troops and lost opportunities, their one great chance of defeating Napoleon in this campaign being lost. If they had made better use of their superiority in cavalry, they would have been aware of Ney's dispositions. If these crucial early attacks had been pressed home with vigour they could have utterly routed Ney's men before reinforcements arrived. Ney's failure to adequately screen his camp nearly proved a disastrous oversight. Napoleon's speedy reactions to the developing situation turned a dangerous crisis to his advantage and his leadership did much to ensure a French victory here, albeit a hollow one. Napoleon's Marie-Louises had shown great courage, but the losses they suffered, both in battle and on the march, showed just how difficult it would be for Napoleon to win the campaign with this army. The Allies, on the other hand, had faced history's great captain and given him a bloody nose. Their hope was that this would help shake the Austrians off the fence and encourage them to join the new coalition.

The Road from Lützen to Bautzen

The Allied monarchs left the field shortly after 9.00pm believing they could continue the battle the next day. Knowing they faced a larger French force, Wittgenstein advised a withdrawal, however, and this

TOP, RIGHT **Prussian dragoons skirmishing. This interesting engraving shows how cavalry skirmishers operated at this time. Like their infantry counterparts, this was in pairs, one loading while the other fired. The firing figure shows how the horse's reins would be held during this process and how the firer attempted to steady his aim.**

BOTTOM, RIGHT **Cossacks looting. They were as likely to prey on friend as foe, and those areas of Germany supposedly liberated by the Allies suffered from their plundering probably as severely as those in French hands .**

advice was accepted. The Allies chose to retreat via Altenburg and Frohburg to Dresden and Meissen; with the French holding the fortresses of Madgeburg and Wittenberg this was the only practicable route. The border of neutral Austria would protect their left flank and this was the quickest way to the Russian reserves

Covered by the Corps of Eugene of Württemberg and Miloradovich, the army withdrew with the Russians marching via Pegau to Altenburg and Frohburg, while the Prussians and parts of Wintzingerode's cavalry fell back to Frohburg and Borna. On the evening of 3 May two large groups camped at Frohburg and Borna. Württemberg clashed with Macdonald's vanguard about noon before crossing the Pleisse at Lucka. Miloradovich delayed Bertrand's advance by destroying the bridge at Predel. His rearguard remained at Lucka while the main body reached the Pleisse. With their chronic shortage of cavalry it was impossible for the French to carry out a vigorous pursuit.

Count Czernichev, commander of a Russian raiding-party. Several raiding-parties operated across the North German Plain, causing problems for the French occupiers. These parties normally consisted of a mixture of Cossacks and regular cavalry, sometimes with some artillery support.

Freiherr von Tettenborn, the liberator of Hamburg. Forcibly annexed by France in 1810, Hamburg, a major port and trading centre, suffered severely from the Continental System. The arrival of Russian troops early in 1813 was greatly welcomed, but this city fell again to the French, who then ruled the rebellious inhabitants with an iron fist.

Barclay, commanding the Reserve Army, was ordered to move rapidly to join the Main Army. Bülow meanwhile, hearing of the events at Grossgörschen, marched to Rosslau, where he crossed the Elbe. In the following days, the Allies continued their retreat to Dresden and Meissen. The French followed, but the allied cavalry prevented them from taking advantage of the situation. A number of minor actions took place at Colditz, Etzdorf, Wilsdruff and Kesselsdorf. By 6–7 May the Allies had reached the right bank of the Elbe and on 8 May the Russian rearguard crossed the three bridges across the Elbe at Dresden closely pursued by Eugène. Order was however maintained, the retreat did not become a rout and now the Elbe River lay between the two armies.

On the evening of 2 May, Napoleon too had expected the battle to continue the next day and all available troops moved to support him. By the morning of 3 May he had around 120,000 men and 327 guns available and with the numerical odds so heavily in his favour he anticipated a crushing victory. By 9.00am, however, the news of the Allied retreat had reached him and he ordered a pursuit instead. Eugène was ordered to take Macdonald and Latour-Maubourg's cavalry in the direction of Pegau, Lauriston to Zwenkau, and both Marmont and Bertrand to cross the Elster at Lützkewitz and Predel. Napoleon himself rode with the Guard towards Pegau. Ney's exhausted and battered Corps was ordered to clear up the battlefield.

The French crossed the Elster virtually without incident and by the evening of 3 May, Lauriston had reached Peres, Macdonald Pöldelwitz and Wischstauden and Marmont was around Löbnitz and Lützkewitz. Bertrand's Corps was at Predel and the Guard in Pegau. The army had covered about 15 km that day. Oudinot's Corps followed in support with Hammerstein's Westphalian Division, both reaching Naumburg, while Franquemont's Württembergers force marched to Kaja.

That night, Napoleon received information indicating the Allies were retiring towards Dresden in two columns. These sources confirmed that the troops were in good order, but that the Russians and Prussians were blaming each other for the defeat. Napoleon decided to detached a force to the north to cross the Elbe at either Torgau or Wittenberg where they would meet little resistance, while the bulk of his forces were to conduct a close pursuit. Such a threat to their right might persuade the Allies to fall back behind the Oder River. It might also lead to the Prussians and Russians dividing their forces, the Prussians to defend Berlin, their capital, and the Russians their line of communication via Poland.

On 4 May, Ney was ordered to march to Leipzig and from there, depending on circumstances, to either Torgau or Wittenberg. He would be joined by Reynier's VII Corps, which included Durutte's Division, the Saxon troops in Torgau, who were now likely to join Napoleon, Victor's provisional II Corps with its two divisions and Sébastiani's II Cavalry Corps reinforced by Puthod's Division of V Corps. This force numbered about 60,000 infantry, 4,000 cavalry and 129 guns.

The force under Napoleon's direct command consisted of around 120,000 men, 11,500 cavalry and 386 guns. Following up were a further 9,000 infantry, 4,800 cavalry and 48 guns.

On 4 May, the French advanced on a broad front, making up for lost time with forced marches. The right column under Bertrand crossed the Elbe at Predel, reaching Dresden on 9 May without coming into contact

The Cossack raid on Berlin, 20 February 1813. This particular raid struck fear into the French garrison of Prussia's capital, but it would be a few more weeks before Napoleon's men had to abandon their hold on this city.

with the Allies. The left column under Lauriston reached Meissen on 8 May and also met only light resistance. Only Macdonald's Corps had to fight its way towards Dresden. Marmont and the Guard followed, making a total of 54,000 men marching down one road. By the evening of 8 May Macdonald's vanguard, the Old Guard and Marmont's Corps were in and around Dresden, Bertrand in Potschappel and Tharandt, Lauriston before Meissen and the remainder of the army to the rear. Although Napoleon was urging on his men, his Marie-Louises could not keep up the pace required. The numbers of hungry marauders and footsore deserters grew daily.

Ney reached Torgau, whose Saxon garrison under General von Thielemann, lacking orders, refused to open the gates of the fortress to him, thus denying him the crossing of the Elbe. Ney took up positions nearby and prepared to throw a bridge across the river at Belgern. On

7 May, Napoleon sent a message to King Frederick August of Saxony, who was in Prague, part of the Austrian Empire, demanding to be given command of the two regiments of heavy cavalry accompanying the King and the opening of the fortresses of Torgau and Königstein. Before the reply arrived, Napoleon received news of Thielemann's response at Torgau. Napoleon then sent an ultimatum to Prague, demanding Frederick August meet his obligations as a member of the Confederation of the Rhine. The King acceded to these demands and sent a letter of apology to Napoleon. He then ordered Thielemann to open the gates of Torgau to the French. Thielemann quit Saxon service in disgust. Napoleon had now secured a vital fortified crossing of the Elbe.

Napoleon arrived in Dresden and found that certain crossing points were in range of the Russian artillery, so French pontooniers used the

Cossacks clash with the French garrison of Berlin at the Halle Gate, 4 March 1813. Berlin fell to the Russians shortly afterwards.

cover of darkness on 8/9 May to throw a bridge across the Elbe. A detachment of troops secured the bridgehead and although the Russians counter-attacked on the morning of 9 May a French grand battery of 80 guns drove off Miloradovich's men, forcing them to fall back towards Bautzen. By the morning of 10 May, Neustadt was in French hands. The damaged stone bridge was repaired while infantry crossed the river on barges. This work was completed in 16 hours, allowing XI, IV and VI Corps to start crossing the Elbe from the morning of 11 May. That afternoon, one of Macdonald's light cavalry divisions moved down the road to Bautzen. Meanwhile, Bertrand's Corps advanced towards Königsbrück and Marmont's vanguard reached Reichenberg, making contact with the Allies. Macdonald's advance continued in the face of stiff resistance from the Russians, reaching Schmiedefeld on 11 May and Bischofswerda the next day. Bertrand reached Kamenz and Königsbrück on 12 May with little delay. Here, covering a line from Bischofswerda through Kamenz to Königsbrück, Macdonald and Bertrand halted, awaiting further orders.

By the evening of 11 May, Napoleon had crossed the Elbe at Dresden with 70,000 men and at Torgau with 45,000. His troops were having difficulty maintaining such a pace and his army was slowly disintegrating. Furthermore, he was uncertain of the Allies' intentions, so he halted his army to rest and restore order. The chance of the decisive victory he was seeking was slowly slipping away.

Indecision at Allied Headquarters

After having retired across the Elbe, a cloud of indecision again descended on the Allies. If they were to convince the Austrians to join the coalition they would have to face Napoleon on the battlefield again. On 7 May Wittgenstein proposed taking up a position between Herzberg

The bridge across the Elbe at Dresden after its destruction on 19 March 1813. Eugène was, by this time, falling back on the line of the Elbe, which he hoped to hold until Napoleon arrived. He blew out one arch of this important bridge over the river to prevent the Russians from crossing it. The advancing French later repaired the bridge.

and Luckau from where he could hit the French as they came over the Elbe. Appropriate orders were issued on 8 May and the Russians took up positions north of Meissen, while the Prussians deployed to the south. Kleist held the bridge at Mühlberg and Cossacks observed the entire right bank of the Elbe with orders to report any French move. Early on 9 May the Russians took positions around Radeberg, the Prussians at Grossenhain. However, despite Wittgenstein's expressed wishes, Miloradovich engaged the French at Übigau and was forced back, leading Wittgenstein to consider a further withdrawal. The chance to seriously delay the French crossing of the Elbe was lost. Further

Generallieutnant Gerhard Johann David von Scharnhorst (1755-1813). Son of a Hanoverian cavalry sergeant, Scharnhorst was one of the great military minds and reformers of this period. Recruited to the Prussian army, he served as Blücher's chief-of-staff at Lützen, where he received what became a fatal wound. Not taking time to recover, Scharnhorst's wound became infected and he died nearly two months after the battle. Gneisenau replaced him.

LEFT The founding of the Prussian militia, 17 March 1813. Regarded as an important step in Prussia's uprising in 1813, the militia consisted mainly of untrained youths with a cadre of older officers and NCOs, some of whom had military experience. The militia was not involved in the Spring fighting. (Carl Röchling)

indecision followed until news of the movement of strong French columns on Wittenberg and the preparation of a bridgehead above Torgau arrived on 10 May. Wittgenstein became convinced the main French thrust was to come via Wittenberg, and that the bridgehead at Torgau and the move via Dresden was only a feint. He then decided to move his Russians back to Bischofswerda and the Prussians to Königsbrück from where he would await developments. Should Napoleon press on, then it was Wittgenstein's intention to unite his forces near Bautzen and offer a battle. Should, however, Napoleon move from Wittenberg and Belgern towards Berlin, Wittgenstein could operate against his flank.

However, on 11 May this plan also had to be scrapped. News arrived of French movements towards Bautzen, Königsbrück and Reichenberg, and Napoleon was reported to be in Dresden awaiting the return of Frederick August. Wittgenstein reacted by ordering his troops to concentrate at Bautzen. The rearguard under Miloradovich fell back to Schmiedefeld having fought Macdonald at Weissig, while Kleist withdrew to Kamenz after having been attacked by Bertrand around Königsbrück. On 12 May, Wittgenstein moved to the right bank of the Spree River at Bautzen and Miloradovich held off Bertrand at Schmiedefeld before also retiring to Bautzen. By 15 May, the French had taken control of the left bank of the Spree.

Napoleon Loses Contact with the Allies

While the Allies pondered, uncertain of Napoleon's intentions, Napoleon was equally uncertain of their intentions. Lacking cavalry, he lost contact with the Allied army and began to receive confusing reports. When he heard that the Russians were falling back to Bischofswerda and the Prussians to Königsbrück, Napoleon believed the Allies were moving apart. His hope was increased by reports of differences between the Allies. The precise situation was not clear however, so Napoleon waited a few days, using the time to restore order in his army. The sickness rate was high due to the lack of supplies and the great exertions of recent days. Food and ammunition were brought up, field hospitals established and the lines of communication secured against Allied raiding parties. The fortifications at Dresden were improved and the garrisons of Wittenberg and Torgau strengthened. The restoration of order and the arrival of reinforcements brought Napoleon's strength up to 200,000 men.

With the condition of his army now improving, Napoleon's objectives began to crystallise. He wanted to move against Glogau, Breslau and Berlin, allowing Davoût to recapture Hamburg and advance into Pomerania. Ney was ordered to Luckau, from where he could either move on Berlin or go to aid Napoleon. On the morning of 12 May, the situation began to clarify. Bertrand reported that the Prussians were falling back from Königsbrück towards Bautzen and that evening was able to add that no Prussians troops were moving on Berlin. Bautzen also appeared to be the point of concentration of the Russian Army. Rumours were heard that Barclay had marched into Guben on 11 May and although these reports were unconfirmed, they led Napoleon to move up the Imperial Guard and Oudinot Corps. Furthermore, Victor was ordered to march from Wittenberg to Luckau while Ney was to move from Torgau to Luckau. Reynier was to maintain contact with these two

columns, while Lauriston was to march to Dobrilugk on 16 May. Napoleon hoped that by 15 May he would be in a position to decide on his next move.

On 14 May, both Marmont and Bertrand received reports that the Allies concentrating at Bautzen were digging in. Napoleon could no longer entertain hopes of dividing the allied forces and defeating them in detail. Nevertheless, Napoleon considered it unlikely that the Allies would offer battle at Bautzen should Ney move against their right, and did not order him up. He wanted to confirm they were intending to make a stand at Bautzen and sent off Bertrand to probe their positions and, if possible, to occupy the town of Bautzen itself. Marmont's Corps, at Bischofswerda, was to be ready to move to his aid. Bertrand was to draw up in echelons between Königsbrück and Kamenz, while Oudinot moved up along the road from Fischbach to Bischofswerda. These movements were executed on 14 and 15 May, leading to heavy fighting with the Russian rearguard.

By the evening of 15 May, Macdonald's Corps was at Klein-Förstgen, 4 km from Bautzen while the Imperial Guard and Reserve Artillery were in and around Dresden. Ney meanwhile had his Corps at Luckau while Lauriston was around Dobrilugk and Sonnenwalde, Reynier at Annaburg and Löben and Victor was crossing the Elbe at Wittenberg.

Napoleon now decided to cancel his move against Berlin and unite all his forces to attack the Allies in their chosen and prepared position at Bautzen. His hope was to bring on the decisive engagement of the campaign. Victor and Reynier were ordered to Bautzen and on the evening of 17 May, Ney reported he would have II, III, V and VIII Corps there by 21 May. Napoleon moved up his main body to tie down the Allies and not allow them to move away. A number of clashes took place between the outposts. By the evening of 19 May, Napoleon had his headquarters at Hartau accompanied by the Old Guard, the Reserve Artillery and the Guard Cavalry. Ney's vanguard under Kellermann reached Wartha, his main body Maukendorf, and Lauriston was at Weissig.

Reynier and Victor's orders had been delayed and they had only reached Alt-Döbern and Finsterwalde and would not be able to reach Bautzen for the battle on 20 and 21 May.

The Allies Decide to Fight at Bautzen

The Allied decision to fight at Bautzen was based on certain assumptions. It was assumed that the French forces would approach from the direction of Dresden and that their superiority in numbers would have been diminished by losses both from the fighting and the marching, and by the need to secure the line of communications. Finally, it was hoped that the arrival of Allied reinforcements would ensure that the difference in numbers would be significantly less than at the Battle of Lützen. A position was to be prepared across the Spree, while the walled town of Bautzen would form the main position. Moreover, the heights to the south of Bautzen would form the anchor-point of the left flank, while the right would be secured on terrain that was marshy with numerous lakes.

Good though this position may have looked on the map, a close examination of the ground revealed several weaknesses. Only in a few places was the right bank of the Spree higher than the left, giving the advantage to the French artillery. Furthermore, the river was easily fordable in several places, making its line difficult to defend. The position originally selected was thus considered unsuitable and a new position selected, three to four kilometres to the east. Here, the terrain was hilly, sloping gently down towards the Spree with several villages which made ideal defensive positions. The left flank was protected by the wooded heights at Klein-Kunitz, whose proximity to the Austrian border made them virtually impenetrable. The right flank rested on the bastion-like Kreckwitz hills, which also appeared to offer the possibility of hiding strong reserves for a counter-attack against the French left.

The Combat at Merseburg, 29 April 1813. Volunteers and musketeers of the 1st East Prussian Infantry Regiment defending the bridge over the Saale. This important bridge was on one of the routes leading to Leipzig, Napoleon's objective at this stage of the campaign. The French forced the Allies to abandon it to them.

View from the Monarch's Hill towards Grossgörschen. Ney's Corps bivouacked in these fields on the night of 1/2 May 1813. From this vantagepoint, the Allies were able to observe them while moving up their own troops behind the cover of a ridge. (Photo courtesy of Ed Wimble of Clash-of-Arms)

Furthermore, it was not intended to let Napoleon cross the Spree unopposed. Forward positions running from the Thromberg to Nieder-Gurig along the Spree were examined. Here, the first resistance could be offered. The strongpoint was the town of Bautzen, which was difficult to attack from the side on the Spree. From 14 May, engineers, farm labourers and detachments of troops built numerous earthworks and batteries as well as laying obstacles.

The planned deployments placed Kleist on the right flank in the forward position along the heights running from Burk to Doberschau, with Miloradovich's newly formed 'vanguard of the left flank' covering the left of the forward position. Prince Gortschakoff's 'Battle Corps', formed from Berg's Corps and parts of Miloradovich's, was deployed in a line from Rieschen through Jenkwitz to Baschütz, with Blücher holding the line from Baschütz to the Weissenberg road and Yorck from the Weissenberg road to Litten. The second line consisted of the Russian Guards, Grenadiers and Cuirassiers. The 3rd Army of the West under Barclay de Tolly was to form up on the right flank at the Kreckwitz heights.

This position was strong against any attack coming from the west, but at around 11 kilometres the length of the front was too great for the men available to defend it. The broken terrain would prevent the Allies from using their superior numbers of cavalry to full advantage and the terrain also obstructed any possible line of retreat. These disadvantages were counter-balanced by the preparations made and the number of artillery pieces available in the batteries constructed. However, were this position to be attacked from the north as well as or instead of the west, then it would become untenable. Such an attack would force the right flank to extend an already over-extended front by another five kilometres. The Kreckwitz heights were the key to the position. Their possession would decide the battle.

By 16 May, with the arrival of Barclay de Tolly the Allies had 146 infantry battalions, 195 squadrons of cavalry – a total of 92,000 men – and 622 guns, plus around 4,000 Cossacks. While the men were confident and in good spirits, the relationships in headquarters had further deteriorated. Wittgenstein's suitability was under question. Furthermore, the arrival of the more senior Barclay led Wittgenstein to request removal from his post. The Czar prevaricated, but now interfered in Wittgenstein's decisions more than ever. Wittgenstein's voluminous disposition for the forthcoming battle, dated 19 May, left much to be desired. Certain points were not phrased clearly, and some troops were not even mentioned. Wittgenstein had no contingency plan for an attack from the north and underestimated the delays the difficult terrain would cause to the movement of reinforcements. Furthermore, he took no account of the possibility that Napoleon would use his superior numbers to tie down the allied troops, preventing them from moving to support each other.

Bautzen – Ney Approaches

From 14 May, the outposts of both sides faced each other uneasily, but it was not until 18 May that a forward movement of the French outposts led the Allies to expect a major assault on their positions. The attack did not materialise and a strong Allied reconnaissance showed the French were simply repositioning.

More importantly however was the arrival on 18 May of a report that patrols to the north and on the left bank of the Spree had observed strong French forces around Grossenhain. A letter had been intercepted from Berthier to Bertrand which indicated that these men were the vanguard of Lauriston's Corps. On 18 May, they were in Hoyerswerda and Ney's 18,000 men were only a day's march behind them. It was clear Napoleon was awaiting the arrival of these troops before launching his assault. Moreover, Ney's line of march would put him in a position to strike the Allied right flank, making their position untenable.

The Allies faced the choice either to withdraw or attempt to defeat one of the two French forces before they could unite. A withdrawal would damage morale and the Allies needed some sort of battlefield success to encourage the vacillating Austrians. By 19 May, however, the prospects of a successful attack had diminished somewhat. Napoleon had now concentrated his forces and although the Allies would have the

View from the Monarch's Hill towards the road from Starsiedel to Kaja. In terrain as flat and as open as this, the Allies were able to make use of their superiority in numbers of cavalry, forcing any advancing French infantry on to the defensive. (Photo courtesy of Ed Wimble of Clash-of-Arms)

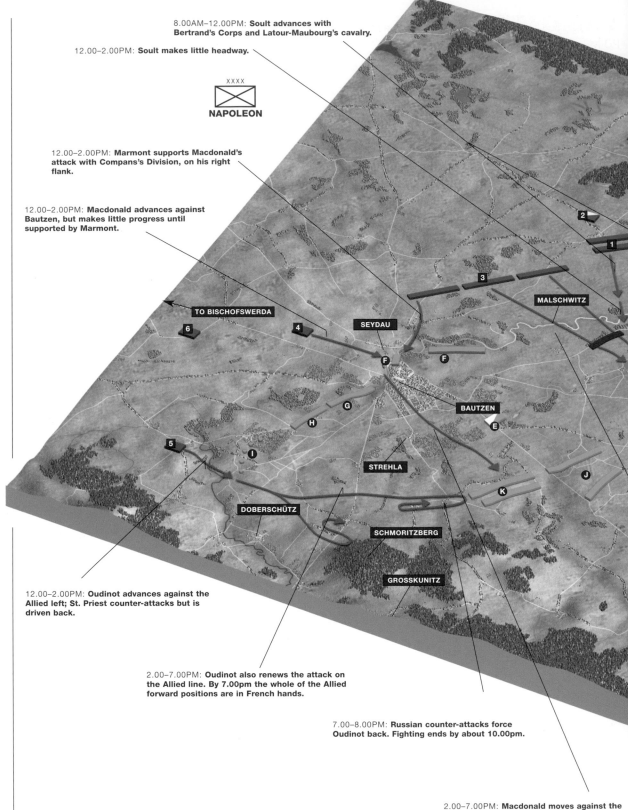

8.00AM–12.00PM: Soult advances with Bertrand's Corps and Latour-Maubourg's cavalry.

12.00–2.00PM: Soult makes little headway.

XXXX

NAPOLEON

12.00–2.00PM: Marmont supports Macdonald's attack with Compans's Division, on his right flank.

12.00–2.00PM: Macdonald advances against Bautzen, but makes little progress until supported by Marmont.

2

1

3

MALSCHWITZ

TO BISCHOFSWERDA

6

4

SEYDAU

F

F

G

BAUTZEN

H

E

5

I

STREHLA

J

K

DOBERSCHÜTZ

SCHMORITZBERG

12.00–2.00PM: Oudinot advances against the Allied left; St. Priest counter-attacks but is driven back.

GROSSKUNITZ

2.00–7.00PM: Oudinot also renews the attack on the Allied line. By 7.00pm the whole of the Allied forward positions are in French hands.

7.00–8.00PM: Russian counter-attacks force Oudinot back. Fighting ends by about 10.00pm.

2.00–7.00PM: Macdonald moves against the Allied front line.

THE BATTLE OF BAUTZEN

20 May 1813, 8.00am–7.00pm, viewed from the south east showing action during the first day of the battle including the early attacks by Soult, Oudinot and Macdonald, and the main French attack from 2.00pm onwards.

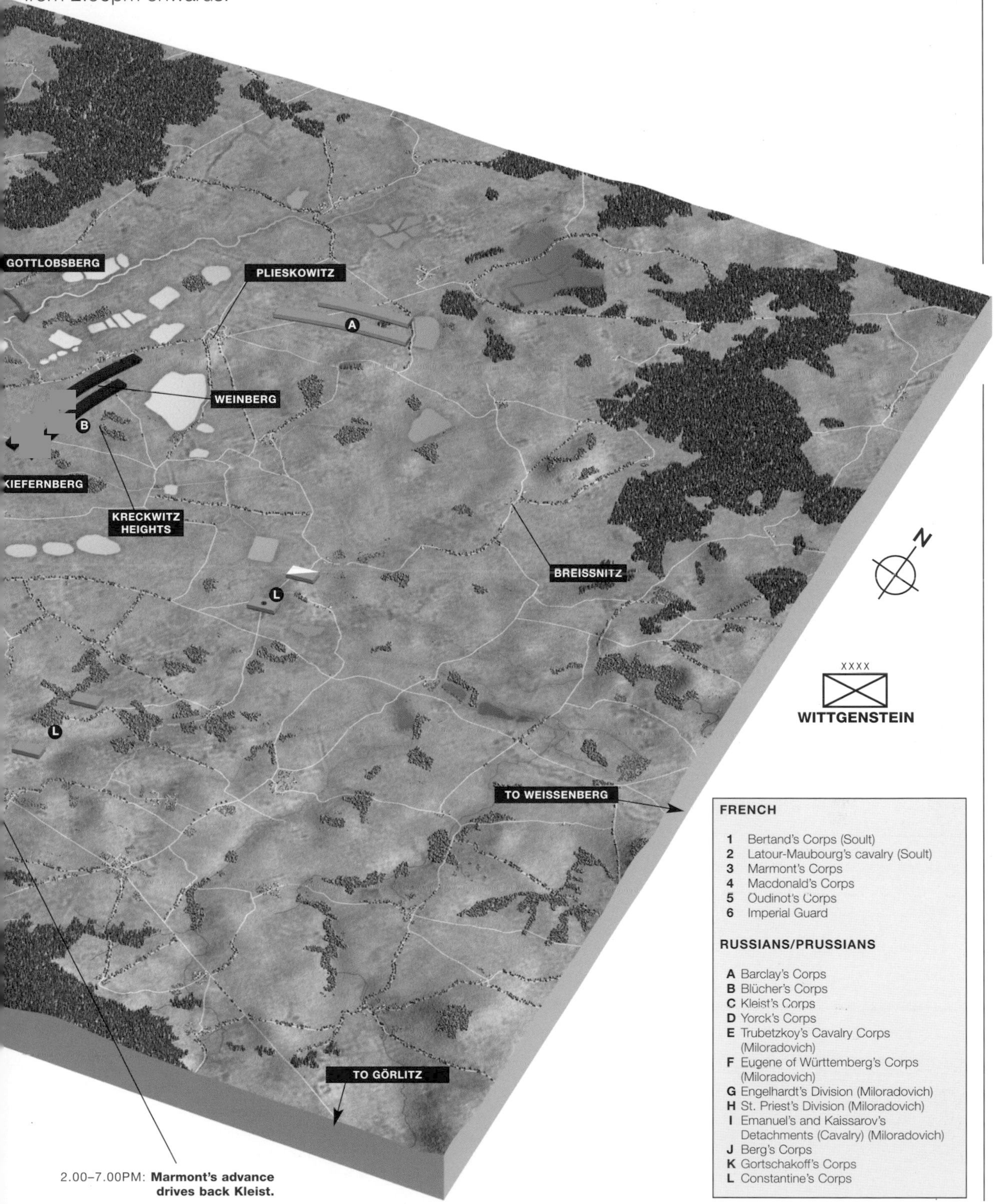

GOTTLOBSBERG

PLIESKOWITZ

A

WEINBERG

B

KIEFERNBERG

KRECKWITZ
HEIGHTS

L

BREISSNITZ

N

xxxx
WITTGENSTEIN

L

TO WEISSENBERG

TO GÖRLITZ

2.00–7.00PM: **Marmont's advance
drives back Kleist.**

FRENCH

1 Bertand's Corps (Soult)
2 Latour-Maubourg's cavalry (Soult)
3 Marmont's Corps
4 Macdonald's Corps
5 Oudinot's Corps
6 Imperial Guard

RUSSIANS/PRUSSIANS

A Barclay's Corps
B Blücher's Corps
C Kleist's Corps
D Yorck's Corps
E Trubetzkoy's Cavalry Corps
    (Miloradovich)
F Eugene of Württemberg's Corps
    (Miloradovich)
G Engelhardt's Division (Miloradovich)
H St. Priest's Division (Miloradovich)
I Emanuel's and Kaissarov's
    Detachments (Cavalry) (Miloradovich)
J Berg's Corps
K Gortschakoff's Corps
L Constantine's Corps

advantage of surprise, they were reluctant to take on the Emperor himself. An attack on Ney, and particularly on Lauriston's column, offered a greater chance of success.

At 1.00am on 19 May, Barclay de Tolly's three columns moved off, made up of the Russian Grenadiers and Yorck's Corps, a total of 24,000 men. Around 1.00pm that afternoon Barclay's columns made contact with the French, but not with Lauriston's vanguard as was expected. Instead, they clashed with Peyri's Italian division, which had moved to join Ney. Surprising the Italians, Tschaplitz's vanguard threw them back to their main positions in Königswartha. Bringing up his main body he was quickly able to drive back the Italians, who were deployed in battle order. The Cossacks pursued them to Wartha, where Ney's vanguard had arrived. Peyri lost 2,680 men including 750 prisoners, all his generals were wounded and he also lost five guns to the Russians, who themselves suffered only 900 casualties.

Yorck contacted Lauriston's vanguard just outside Hermsdorf at about 3.00pm. Barclay had ordered Yorck to march via Hermsdorf to Weissig and Wartha and from there to attack Lauriston in the flank. However, on leaving Hermsdorf Yorck unexpectedly encountered Lauriston just as he received a conflicting order to march on Johnsdorf. Yorck moved four battalions, four squadrons and one battery, under Lieutenant-Colonel von Steinmetz, into a good position on the heights at Weissig and to its south-west, from where they could cover his march to Johnsdorf. On receiving news of the contact made with Lauriston, Barclay ordered Yorck to hold on to these heights until nightfall, sending him one division of the Grenadier Corps in support, and another towards Neu-Steinitz. Yorck's main body, already on its way to Johnsdorf, now retraced its steps. As Steinmetz had already abandoned his position,

The church at Kleingörschen. The level of damage suffered by the buildings of the villages contested in this battle is unclear, but a solid stone-built church was certainly less vulnerable than the timber-framed dwellings. (Photo courtesy of Ed Wimble of Clash-of-Arms)

Prince William of Prussia at Grossgörschen, 2 May 1813. Brother of the King of Prussia, William narrowly escaped becoming a casualty when his horse was shot from under him. (Richard Knötel)

Yorck had to find a new, less favourable one, south-west of Weissig. He was forced to face Lauriston at a disadvantage, but the arrival of the Russian reinforcements enabled him to hang on until nightfall. Barclay then ordered a withdrawal and Yorck fell back to Klix that night. Yorck had lost 1,100 men, Lauriston 1,700. Ney had been strongly checked and he now wanted to await the arrival of Reynier before attempting to advance again. However, other than causing Ney some anxiety, this foray achieved little for the Allies other than to weaken their already outnumbered forces – the two night marches resulted in the loss of 2,000 stragglers.

THE BATTLE OF BAUTZEN

Day One, 20 May 1813

The 19th of May had been relatively quiet for Napoleon's forces, with only some cavalry skirmishing around Dahlowitz and Qualitz between Franquemont and Kleist. The morning of 20 May was also quiet. At 8.00am Napoleon issued orders for the attack, but their execution was delayed while communications with Ney's force, broken since the rout of Peyri's Division, were re-established. Marshal Soult took Bertrand's Corps and Latour-Maubourg's cavalry halfway to Gross-Welka and Klix to support Ney in case he met serious resistance. However, at 9.00am, before Soult had moved off, a report came in from Ney stating that the Allies at Königswartha had fallen back. Ney was ordered to continue his advance to Klix and concentrate his forces there that evening to be able to cross the Spree the next day.

The mortal wounding of Prince Leopold of Hesse-Homburg at the side of General Zieten at Grossgörschen. He was shot through the heart at close range during the street fighting. (Richard Knötel)

Napoleon waited until noon before ordering the attack to allow Ney to get closer. Oudinot was to cross the Spree south of Bautzen and attack the heights opposite. Macdonald and Marmont were to advance on the town of Bautzen itself, while Soult was to move Bertrand against the heights of Burk. For the time being, the Guard was to remain in reserve behind Macdonald.

Facing the French across the Spree was the Allied army with Kleist's Corps on their right flank on the heights at Burk. He had 5,000 men and 39 guns, and had pushed some infantry, four squadrons of cavalry and two guns forward to cover the river crossing at Nieder-Gurig with Russian Jägers occupying Burk. South of Kleist was Duke Eugene of Württemberg – 5,500 men and 12 guns – with his left flank resting against Bautzen and Wolff's Brigade of four battalions with four guns in Bautzen itself. South of Bautzen near Preuschwitz were the 1,050 men and 12 guns of Engelhardt's Brigade with St. Priest's Division – 3,300 men and 12 guns – south of him strung out as far as Doberschau. To St. Priest's rear were the 15 squadrons, 2 Cossack regiments and 12 guns of Prince Trubetzkoi's Cavalry Corps. On the left flank of the Allied army, to the south of St. Priest, around Singwitz and Postwitz, was the light cavalry of Emanuel and Kaissarov (2,400 sabres, 6 guns). These formations had outposts on the left bank of the Spree.

Napoleon's aim was to draw the Allies' attention away from their right flank, so he sent Oudinot's three divisions, supported by one of Latour-Maubourg's cavalry brigades, a total of 18,000 men and 48 guns, to attack Singwitz on the allied left. The Russian cavalry detachments here could do little to slow his advance. St. Priest's Division rushed up, but Pacthod threw him back, first to Boblitz, then to Falkenberg. Here, St. Priest was joined by 2,200 cavalry and twelve guns from Gortschakoff's Corps, enough men to bring Pacthod's advance to a halt. Oudinot diverted Lorencez to Pielitz and Mehltheuer, a move around the Russian left flank he hoped would force them to abandon their position. In the event, it did. St. Priest fell back to the heights at Rabitz and the Russian cavalry to Riechen and Döhlen. A battery in a commanding position on the hill to the rear of Mehltheuer prevented the French from advancing further.

Macdonald's 15,000 men and their 58 guns moved off a little after Oudinot. His leading division under Charpentier found the stone bridge at Bautzen intact and was able to cross the Spree with minimal losses but could make no progress against the town itself. Gérard and Fressinet moved towards Grubschütz intending to circle around Bautzen from the south. Here their advance stalled and Macdonald could only continue once Marmont's attack from the north of Bautzen cleared the way.

Marmont's Corps – 18,600 men and 73 guns – moved off towards the Spree at 1.00p.m. He immediately deployed a battery of 60 guns along the ridge between Teichnitz and Öhna. Its fire drove back the Russian skirmishers, allowing Marmont, under cover of his own skirmishers, to cross the river quickly. He did this by fording the river in some places and in addition by throwing three temporary bridges across it. Compans' Division, on his right flank, then moved against Bautzen, quickly penetrating the northern part of the town. His two other divisions attacked Eugene of Württemberg's positions.

About 4.00p.m. Miloradovich began to fall back and Duke Eugene of Württemberg also staged a fighting withdrawal, reaching his position along the ridge between Auritz and Jenkwitz by 6.00p.m. Macdonald continued to press forward, his advance constantly contested and slowed by the Russians.

Soult's Corps was making little headway against Kleist, despite having a considerable numerical advantage with 17,800 men and 49 guns.

The Prussian Foot Guards storming a village. The quadrangle of four villages that formed the central part of this battle changed hands on several occasions. The bitter fighting must have taken place over the bodies of the dead, dying and wounded, but this later artist sanitised the scene. (Richard Knötel)

'Vive l'Empereur'. Napoleon appears on the battlefield of Grossgörschen, inspiring his Marie-Louises in their bitter fight for the four villages in the centre of this battlefield. Napoleon's personal charisma did much to hold together his inexperienced army.

Unable to cross the Spree, at 3.00pm he ordered Franquemont and Morand to advance in three columns against Gottlobsberg, Nieder-Gurig and Briesing, which they did under fire from Kleist's artillery. Gottlobsberg was soon taken, but the allied cavalry prevented a further advance in the direction of the Kiefern hill. Nieder-Gurig fell at 6.00pm after bitter fighting but the Allies did not hold Briesing and the third French column was able advance on Plieskowitz that afternoon. Marmont's successes cleared the way for Bertrand to continue his advance. However, Marmont failed to take Burk, but Friedrich's Division was able to drive the Allies out of Nieder-Kaina. At around 7.00pm, with the entire Allied forward positions in French hands and in danger of being cut off, Kleist retired to Litten. Soult's attack that evening on Doberschütz and Plieskowitz was driven off.

The advance of Lorencez's Division on the far left had caused the Allies some concern. The Czar and all of his senior officers with the exception of Wittgenstein believed this to be Napoleon's main thrust, so Gortschakoff was ordered to counter-attack with part of the centre and reserves. He did so between 7.00 and 8.00pm, St Priest's attack inflicting heavy losses on Pacthod between Binnewitz and Grubditz. Lorencez was forced to retire to Denkwitz, the fighting here finally ending by 10.00pm.

While the fighting raged around Bautzen that day, Ney was force-marching towards Klix, where that evening he was greeted by Tschaplitz's vanguard. Souham's Division was thrown in immediately against the village, and, after a bitter struggle, it forced the Russians to retire across the Spree. As darkness fell Ney's Corps bivouacked between Stier and Oppitz.

Reflections on Day One

The first day at Bautzen had gone relatively well for Napoleon. True he had suffered losses of around 5,600 men, but he had forced the line of the Spree, prevented the Allies from withdrawing, taken their front line and obtained a good position from which to continue the battle the next day. To the north Ney was now in a position to descend on the Allied right the next day, giving the Emperor the decisive victory he sought. Reports arriving that night from Oudinot and Macdonald indicated that the allies were moving substantial forces against them and would probably mount a concerted counter-attack the next morning. Napoleon could have hoped for nothing better. His feint against the Allied left had seized their attention and was drawing in their reserves. The next morning he would again attack the Allied left with Macdonald, Marmont and Bertrand, hopefully drawing in further reserves and leaving the Allied right more exposed than ever. Once Ney had crossed the Spree at Klix, he was to march on Preititz and the rear of the allied positions. With Ney in their rear Napoleon would attack along the entire Allied front line. The gods of war appeared to be smiling on him once again.

In the Allied camp there was little reason for satisfaction with that day's results. They had made Napoleon pay a price for crossing the Spree, but had failed to launch a counter-attack to drive him back. French reinforcements were moving up and would exacerbate the numerical disparity the next day, and lurking somewhere to the north of them was Ney. The Allies did not know the true strength of his force. If they had they would have seen the danger they were in.

Day Two, 21 May 1813

At 5.00am Napoleon rode to the heights in front of Bautzen on his right flank and saw that the battle had already commenced. At daybreak, the Russians had attacked along the line from Falkenberg to the Thromberg, throwing back Oudinot's vanguard. At 6.00am on Napoleon's orders Oudinot counter-attacked, sending Lorencez's Division against the village of Mehltheuer and Pacthod's against Daranitz. His third division, Raglovich's Bavarians, followed up in

Combat at Königswartha-Weissig, 19 May 1813. This was one of several rearguard actions during the Allied withdrawal to Bautzen.

reserve. Macdonald moved up along the line Jessnitz–Auritz in support. Oudinot's superiority in numbers forced back the Russians, with St Priest taking up positions along the ridge between Rieschen and Klein-Jenkwitz while Pacthod forced Engelhardt's Brigade out of Daranitz. Macdonald was now able to place his artillery on the heights between Daranitz and Rabitz from where he could engage the Allied artillery. The ensuing duel lasted until about 10.00am with the French gaining the upper hand.

After a bombardment, Pacthod stormed the village of Rieschen. For a while the Russians managed to hold their own, but eventually sheer weight of numbers told and Rieschen fell to the French. At the same time Lorencez advanced on Mehltheuer, taking the village from the Russians, and from there pushed on, capturing Gross-Kunitz, Döhlen and Pielitz. By 11.00am the entire Allied left had been forced back and in places Macdonald had even worked his way into the rear of their positions.

These events underlined the Czar's belief that this was the main French thrust, and Ney's threat to the Allied right had yet to become apparent. He therefore ordered, against Wittgenstein's wishes, twelve battalions and 24 guns from the Grenadier Corps to reinforce the Allied left. Shortly after 11.00am, Miloradovich had sufficient men available to stage a counter-attack, driving back Lorencez's weakened force and quickly recapturing Döhlen, Pielitz and Gross-Kunitz. The Russian cavalry charged the retreating French several times, causing disorder and taking several hundred prisoners and one gun. The French eventually retired to the Thromberg. Duke Eugene of Württemberg moved up at the same time, throwing Pacthod out of Rieschen and Daranitz and forcing him to fall back to Binnewitz. Macdonald's artillery was also forced to retire to its original position.

Oudinot's position was now critical; Pacthod's and Lorencez's Divisions had been put to flight, Raglovich was committed and Cossacks were moving on his rear and threatening his artillery park. His calls to Napoleon for reinforcement went unheeded. St Priest's infantry next assaulted Pacthod's and Lorencez's positions along the heights of Binnewitz and the Thromberg, while Russian cavalry moved around them towards Ebendörfel. When Oudinot again asked for urgent assistance Napoleon responded, telling him the battle would be won by 3.00pm and he was to hold his positions until then. Oudinot abandoned his artillery park at Singwitz, falling back to a line from Ebendörfel to Grubditz. An attack by Macdonald's right flank division against the Russians helped ease the pressure. Oudinot held his own until 3.00pm when he received news of the Emperor's victory. The Russian assaults ceased shortly afterwards and when around 4.30pm they began to withdraw, Oudinot attempted to follow up, but his men were too exhausted to move far.

While the French right flank was taking a pounding from the Russian assaults, Napoleon's centre – Marmont, Latour-Maubourg's cavalry and the Imperial Guard – held its positions. At 7.00am a report from Ney arrived acknowledging receipt of his orders to advance via Baruth and Weissenberg, but asking for confirmation as he could hear the sound of guns coming from Hochkirch and Bautzen. Fearing Ney would arrive too late, Napoleon ordered him to march on Preititz, sending Lauriston to outflank the Allied right. Ney's arrival in Preititz would be the signal for an attack along the entire front. The spire of the church in Hochkirch was to be Ney's directional marker. At the same time, Napoleon ordered Soult to be prepared to launch Bertrand's three divisions against the Allies to hold the ground between Ney and Marmont.

Marmont drew up along the right, east of Bautzen and awaited events. At 9.00am he moved to the right to be ready to support Soult and Ney. Soult, whose men were largely still on the left bank of the Spree, engaged the Allies with his artillery for the time being, his attempts to bridge the river delayed by deep water.

The town of Bautzen. On a steep hill with solid buildings, this represented a formidable obstacle that the French eventually bypassed on 20 May, forcing the Allied troops holding it to withdraw.

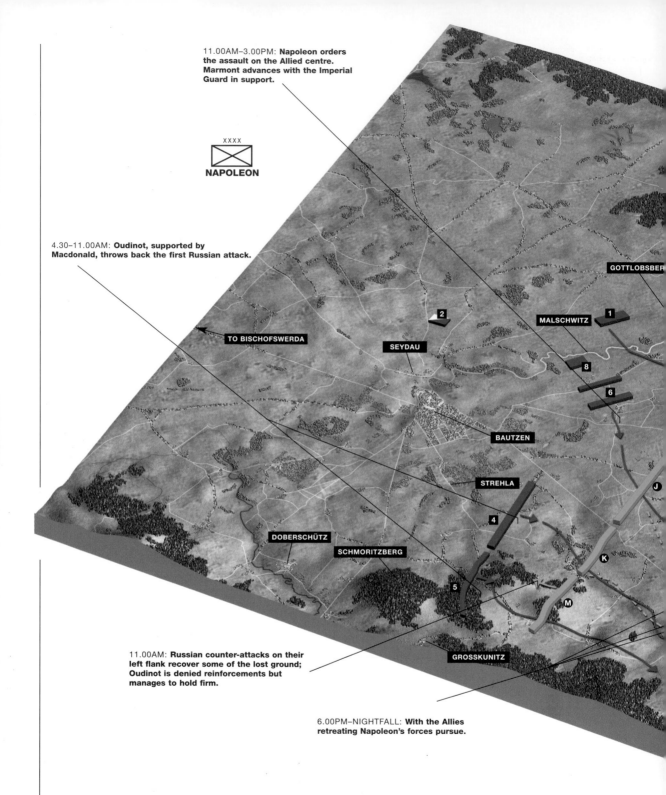

11.00AM–3.00PM: Napoleon orders the assault on the Allied centre. Marmont advances with the Imperial Guard in support.

XXXX
NAPOLEON

4.30–11.00AM: Oudinot, supported by Macdonald, throws back the first Russian attack.

TO BISCHOFSWERDA

GOTTLOBSBER

MALSCHWITZ | 1

2

8

6

SEYDAU

BAUTZEN

STREHLA

J

4

DOBERSCHÜTZ

SCHMORITZBERG

K

5

M

11.00AM: Russian counter-attacks on their left flank recover some of the lost ground; Oudinot is denied reinforcements but manages to hold firm.

GROSSKUNITZ

6.00PM–NIGHTFALL: With the Allies retreating Napoleon's forces pursue.

THE BATTLE OF BAUTZEN

21 May 1813, 4.30am–nightfall, viewed from the south east showing the initial Russian counter-attack against Oudinot, Ney's flank march, the final attack of the French Imperial Guard on the centre of the Allied line and the subsequent Allied retreat and French pursuit.

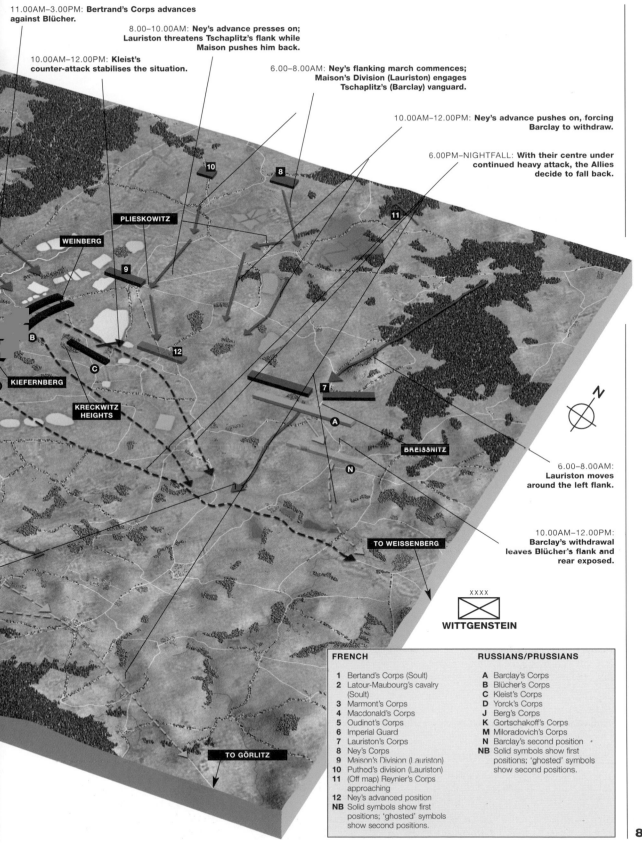

11.00AM–3.00PM: Bertrand's Corps advances against Blücher.

8.00–10.00AM: Ney's advance presses on; Lauriston threatens Tschaplitz's flank while Maison pushes him back.

10.00AM–12.00PM: Kleist's counter-attack stabilises the situation.

6.00–8.00AM: Ney's flanking march commences; Maison's Division (Lauriston) engages Tschaplitz's (Barclay) vanguard.

10.00AM–12.00PM: Ney's advance pushes on, forcing Barclay to withdraw.

6.00PM–NIGHTFALL: With their centre under continued heavy attack, the Allies decide to fall back.

PLIESKOWITZ

WEINBERG

KIEFERNBERG

KRECKWITZ HEIGHTS

BREISSNITZ

6.00–8.00AM: Lauriston moves around the left flank.

10.00AM–12.00PM: Barclay's withdrawal leaves Blücher's flank and rear exposed.

TO WEISSENBERG

TO GÖRLITZ

XXXX
WITTGENSTEIN

FRENCH	RUSSIANS/PRUSSIANS
1 Bertand's Corps (Soult)	**A** Barclay's Corps
2 Latour-Maubourg's cavalry (Soult)	**B** Blücher's Corps
3 Marmont's Corps	**C** Kleist's Corps
4 Macdonald's Corps	**D** Yorck's Corps
5 Oudinot's Corps	**J** Berg's Corps
6 Imperial Guard	**K** Gortschakoff's Corps
7 Lauriston's Corps	**M** Miloradovich's Corps
8 Ney's Corps	**N** Barclay's second position
9 Maison's Division (Lauriston)	**NB** Solid symbols show first positions; 'ghosted' symbols show second positions.
10 Puthod's division (Lauriston)	
11 (Off map) Reynier's Corps approaching	
12 Ney's advanced position	
NB Solid symbols show first positions; 'ghosted' symbols show second positions.	

83

Ney's Flank March

On the evening of 20 May, Ney had ordered III and V Corps to prepare to move on Baruth the next morning while Reynier with the VII Corps was to move on Klix as quickly as possible. Hearing cannon-fire on the morning of 21 May, Ney feared his march would take him away from the battle and sought confirmation from the Emperor. At 6.00am Maison's Division of Lauriston's Corps crossed the Spree at Klix. As they pressed on they were engaged by Tschaplitz's vanguard at Salga, forcing Lauriston's two other divisions to move around this position. Kellermann's, Souham's and Delmas' Divisions all moved up in support with Albert's Division remaining in reserve. Tschaplitz was now attacked frontally and his flank threatened and he fell back. Lauriston forced him back further and, attempting to cover Barclay's right flank, Tschaplitz fell back to Gotta (now Guttau). He burned the crossing over the Cannewitz Water, hoping to delay the French advance.

Barclay observed these events from the windmill hill at Gleina and asked the Czar for reinforcements. Alexander sent the Prussian Lieutenant-Colonel von Müffling to confirm the situation, who immediately saw the danger to the Allied right and rushed to Blücher, asking for his support. But before this help could arrive, Ney attacked again, with Lauriston moving against Gotta, Kellermann towards the copse at the Neuer Teich, Souham and Delmas on Gleina and Maison on Malschwitz. The Russians unsuccessfully attempted to drive off the French with heavy artillery fire from the windmill hill, but Lauriston simply moved around the windmill hill, making this position untenable and thereby exposing the line of retreat along the road at Wurschen, so Barclay ordered a withdrawal on Preititz and Buchwalde. Tschaplitz also

A solitary Napoleon draws up his plan of battle for 21 May 1813 under the protective gaze of Old Guardsmen. It was Napoleon's failure to communicate his intentions clearly to Ney that resulted in a delay in the flanking move. This delay allowed the Allies to slip away, costing Napoleon his one real chance of victory.

The Colberg Infantry Regiment fighting for the Kreckwitz Heights on 21 May 1813. They were an important section of the Allied front line on 21 May, and their loss forced a withdrawal.

fell back to Buchwalde, where he endeavoured to hold his positions, the marshy terrain and the numerous ponds helping him delay the French advance. Barclay now withdrew his main body from Preititz to Baruth. Barclay's withdrawal to Preititz did not please the Czar, who had just sent half of his reserves against Oudinot on the opposite flank. He ordered Barclay to hold Preititz to the last man, but by the time the order arrived Barclay was already on his way to Baruth.

Meanwhile, Ney continued to push forwards, taking the windmill hill at Gleina now abandoned by Barclay. With Ricard's and Marchand's Divisions yet to arrive and Maison fully engaged at Malschwitz Ney considered himself too weak to continue the advance immediately. At this moment Napoleon's order instructing him to be in Preititz by 11.00am arrived. Believing he had time to wait for the rest of his men to move up, Ney ordered Lauriston to move to the right and support him at Preititz. While Ney awaited fresh troops the French were pressing forwards either side of him. On the right Maison took Malschwitz, while on the left Lauriston pressed on from Gotta. Tschaplitz, reinforced by men from Barclay and Lanskoi's Detachment, took up positions on the Schafberg, but after a short artillery duel, he withdrew in face of the French assault columns. Lauriston followed up towards Baruth, ignoring Ney's order to move on Preititz, as he believed the marshy terrain would make that impossible.

Barclay's departure from Preititz endangered Blücher's line of retreat, and it was vital the village was quickly regained and held. His forces there were too weak to halt Souham's assault and the village fell to the French at 11.00am. At this moment reinforcements arrived from Blücher's Corps, and three battalions of Roeder's Brigade forced the French back into Preititz. As the rest of Kleist's Corps arrived the Allies could now counter-attack, and after a long struggle Souham was eventually ejected from Preititz and forced to withdraw to the windmill hill at Gleina. Ney now urged Reynier to move up quickly and again ordered Lauriston to move on Preititz. This time, Lauriston obeyed, leaving just Rochambeau's Division and the 3rd Light Cavalry Division facing Barclay's men now drawn up on heights at Briessnitz and Rackel, moving the remainder of his corps towards Preititz.

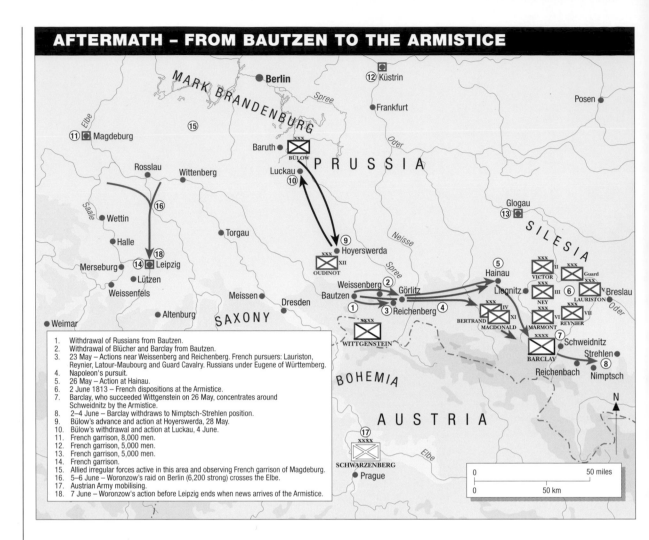

AFTERMATH – FROM BAUTZEN TO THE ARMISTICE

1. Withdrawal of Russians from Bautzen.
2. Withdrawal of Blücher and Barclay from Bautzen.
3. 23 May – Actions near Weissenberg and Reichenberg. French pursuers: Lauriston, Reynier, Latour-Maubourg and Guard Cavalry. Russians under Eugene of Württemberg.
4. Napoleon's pursuit.
5. 26 May – Action at Hainau.
6. 2 June 1813 – French dispositions at the Armistice.
7. Barclay, who succeeded Wittgenstein on 26 May, concentrates around Schweidnitz by the Armistice.
8. 2–4 June – Barclay withdraws to Nimptsch-Strehlen position.
9. Bülow's advance and action at Hoyerswerda, 28 May.
10. Bülow's withdrawal and action at Luckau, 4 June.
11. French garrison, 8,000 men.
12. French garrison, 5,000 men.
13. French garrison, 5,000 men.
14. French garrison.
15. Allied irregular forces active in this area and observing French garrison of Magdeburg.
16. 5–6 June – Woronzow's raid on Berlin (6,200 strong) crosses the Elbe.
17. Austrian Army mobilising.
18. 7 June – Woronzow's action before Leipzig ends when news arrives of the Armistice.

By now Maison had moved forwards from Malschwitz towards Plieskowitz and he forced back the Prussians to the heights at Doberschütz. Ney now threw everyone he had against Preititz. The divisions of Delmas, Ricard and Albert, about 14,000 men, were ordered to recapture Preititz itself, while Puthod, Marchand and Souham, the latter having already suffered heavily, were held in reserve at Gleina. Kleist faced them with 2,500 men and 30 guns, but fell back to the heights at Belgern when he received news of Lauriston's flanking move. Ney was now master of Preititz and nothing could stop him moving on Hochkirch, thereby cutting Blücher's line of retreat. However, instead he now wheeled to the right to attack the Allied positions at Klein-Bautzen.

Events in the Centre

When at 11.00am Napoleon heard artillery fire coming from Preititz he knew Ney had arrived and ordered Marmont to cross the Blösaer Water and attack the Russian centre along the ridge at Nieder-Kaina. Napoleon was not unable to attack along the entire front as he had intended as Soult's crossing of the Spree had met with delays. It was pointless having Marmont attack alone, so the Guard were ordered to take the heights west of Kreckwitz. Mortier was ordered to threaten Blücher but not to get

The 9th Company of the 1st West Prussian Infantry Regiment storming the brickworks at Doberschütz, 21 May 1813. Detailed to protect Prussian artillery positions, this company drove off French skirmishers that were using the cover of the brickworks to fire on the gun teams.

drawn into a fight. With a decisive victory now in his grasp Napoleon sent the news to Paris, Vienna and Cracow.

By 1.00pm Soult's bridge at the Kiefernberg was ready and he could now move to support Bertrand's attack on Blücher's positions. Artillery fire on the Gottlobsberg and the western edge of the Kiefernberg prepared the way and Franquemont's Württemberg Division marched in column towards the Kopatschberg, while two brigades of Morand's Division drove on Plieskowitz and Doberschütz. A third advanced towards the Weisser Stein. The Württembergers faced heavy artillery and threw back a counter-attack by Klüx's Brigade of Prussians. The Prussians fell back to a line running from Doberschütz through Weinberg to Kreckwitz.

Blücher was now under attack from three sides and realised he could no longer hold his positions. He sent a request to Yorck at Litten for support, who in response despatched Steinmetz's Brigade and followed with the rest of his corps once relieved by Yermolof's Russian Guards Division. By now it was too late and faced with annihilation if he attempted to hold his positions, Blücher began to withdraw around 3.00pm His brigades fell back on both sides of Purschwitz and took up new positions on the far side of the Blösaer Water. Yorck retired with them, the Allied cavalry preventing a French pursuit. Yermolof linked up with the withdrawing Prussians at Litten, allowing them to rally, and then followed them to Wurschen.

At around 3.00pm Napoleon moved up a battery of 60 guns to the west of Basankwitz and had it fire on the heights at Kreckwitz. A division of the Young Guard advanced towards Kreckwitz to support Bertrand, but this proved unnecessary as Ney's flanking move was now taking effect. His divisions at Klein-Bautzen linked up with Soult's troops

Marshal Édouard-Adolphe-Casimir-Joseph Mortier, Duke of Treviso (1768-1835), commander of the Imperial Guard in 1813. While the Young Guard engaged in combat at both Lützen and Bautzen, the Old Guard, although present, did not see action.

coming from the Kreckwitz hills. Confusion broke out when Lauriston arrived here as well. It took an hour to restore order, allowing the Allies to make good their withdrawal.

By 4.00pm Barclay on the Allied right faced only Rochambeau's Division at Rackel. In the centre Blücher and Yorck had been forced back across the Blösaer Water from where they could offer little further resistance, and on the left Miloradovich was facing the French reserves to his front and a threat to his left. Any chance of victory had gone and the best that could be hoped for was a safe withdrawal. With Preititz in French hands for a second time, the need to retire was pressing, but Wittgenstein, insulted by the Czar's constant interference, said nothing, so it was left to General von der Knesebeck to issue the order to withdraw. The Allies would withdraw in three columns; the right under Barclay was to hold off the French at Rackel and Briessnitz long enough for the centre column – the Prussians and Yermolof – to fall back beyond Wurschen. The left column under Miloradovich was to fall back on Löbau while the left flank of the centre covered this move at Jenkwitz.

Covered by their cavalry, the Allies withdrew. Exhausted by the day's fighting the French right was in no position to follow up. Now joined by Reynier's Corps and Puthod's Division, the French left advanced cautiously. In the centre Marmont and Macdonald attempted to conduct a more vigorous pursuit, but eight fresh battalions of Russian Guards held them off. Duke Eugene of Württemberg fell back in good order and that evening the Allies were in two columns about 10 km apart, one at Weissenberg, the other at Löbau. The rearguard held positions on the left bank of the Löbauer Water. Ney, Lauriston and Reynier had reached Wurschen; the Imperial Guard were at Purschwitz and Bertrand and Latour-Maubourg had pushed as far as Drehsa and Canitz-Christina. Marmont, Macdonald and Oudinot were in a line from Meschwitz to Waditz. French losses in the two days of fighting amounted to 25,000 men including 3,700 missing of which 800 had been taken prisoner. This compared to Allied losses of 10,850 men.

A decisive victory had again slipped through the French Emperor's fingers. He had suffered double the losses of his enemies only to see them withdraw in good order. Despite a substantial numerical advantage and Ney's bold flanking move, Napoleon had failed to crush the Prusso-Russian forces. This despite the Czar playing into his hands, convinced the main French effort was against the Allied left. Having fought two bloody battles without achieving the crushing victory he so desperately needed to win a respite, time was running out for Napoleon.

The Allies too had lost an opportunity. Fighting on ground of their choosing they failed to hold off Napoleon's forces and win a victory. Lack of clear leadership and dissension and confusion among the high command left the army without a clear strategy and surrendered the initiative to the French. Nevertheless, their army was intact and in good spirits. They had now twice taken on Napoleon in person and given him much to think about, despite being outnumbered and outflanked on both occasions. They had pulled their head out of a noose and their superiority in cavalry prevented any effective French pursuit. If the French legions, with superior numbers and led by their Emperor in person, could not crush the Allies, then with more men, they could bring the 'tyrant' to bay. It was hoped that the determination they had displayed so far would be enough to entice Austria into the new coalition, finally swinging the numerical advantage in their favour.

Bautzen to the Cease-fire

Early on 22 May, the Allied withdrawal continued towards Görlitz on the Oder River. Blücher and Barclay, who had fallen back to Weissenberg the previous evening, altered direction before crossing the Neisse River below Görlitz over a pontoon bridge. The Russians camping at Löbau took the direct route via Reichenbach to Görlitz. From Reichenbach, Miloradovich was to act as the rearguard. A vigorous pursuit was not anticipated.

Napoleon wanted to make up for the lost opportunities on 21 May by leading the pursuit in person. He intended to lead Reynier, Lauriston, Ney, Latour-Maubourg and the Guard on Reichenbach, while Macdonald's and Bertrand's Corps advanced via Hochkirch and Nostitz. Marmont was also to advance via Hochkirch and join with either the left or the right of the army. Victor and Sébastiani were ordered forward as well, but Oudinot's battered Corps would remain on the battlefield.

At daybreak, the two armies clashed again. The artillery of Reynier's vanguard fired on the Allied rearguard under Yermolof and Katzeler at Kotitz, on the heights west of Weissenberg. Napoleon sent the entire Guard Cavalry and Latour-Maubourg around their left while Reynier, supported by Lauriston, moved against their front. Although repeatedly forced back, each time the Russians took up a new position, fighting hard and holding off the pursuers. The French lost both time and men.

At 10.00am the French attacked Nieder-Reichenbach, forcing back two battalions of Russian Jäger with heavy artillery fire. Both sides now deployed cavalry and Reynier advanced again, forcing back the Russians at 3.00pm. The tired French clashed with another Russian rearguard several kilometres east of Reichenbach at 5.00pm, again forcing it to withdraw with flanking moves. Napoleon broke off the pursuit at 7.00pm as his men were exhausted. He took no prisoners, having advanced less than 8 km in one day.

On 23 May, the Allies continued their withdrawal, the rearguard now commanded by Count Pahlen, as Miloradovich was indisposed. The French failed to interrupt the crossing of the Neisse, determined Russians again delaying their pursuit, this time at Leopoldshain. On 24 May there were only minor clashes at Siegersdorf and by the next day the Allies had reached Hainau and Goldberg. Finally, on 26 May, Barclay de Tolly replaced Wittgenstein as commander-in-chief of the Allied army. This was not to be the only good news of the day.

Combat at Hainau, 26 May 1813

Although withdrawing the Allies wanted to underline their determination to carry on the fight. With this in mind Gneisenau, Blücher's chief-of-staff, drew up a plan to surprise and overwhelm part of the pursuing French forces. He had 22 squadrons and three horse batteries under Colonel von Dolffs take up hidden positions in the basin of Baudmannsdorf, while eight and a half battalions, two squadrons and three batteries were placed at Pohlsdorf to cover any eventual retreat.

That day Napoleon intended to attack the Russian rearguard along the road to Löwenberg with Marmont's Corps and Latour-Maubourg's

OVERLEAF **The Destruction of Maison's Division at Hainau, 26 May 1813. Although he enjoyed the advantage of numbers, Napoleon was severely handicapped by a lack of cavalry. He could still win battles, as he showed at Lützen and Bautzen, but he was unable to destroy the beaten army on the retreat with a close and effective pursuit. On the contrary, as the Allies had the larger amount of cavalry, they were able on occasion to turn the tables on the pursuer. The ambush of Maison's Division at Hainau, just a few days after Bautzen, showed that the Allies were far from demoralised. Dolffs, leading several Prussian cavalry regiments, including the Guard Light Cavalry, the East Prussian and Silesian Cuirassiers and the West Prussian Uhlans, rode down a number of French squares, some after a hard fight, some while still in the process of forming. Dolffs fell mortally wounded, but not before having destroyed Maison's Division. (Christa Hook)**

cavalry. As a result of various delays the Prussians had to wait until 5.00pm before Maison's Division with six battalions and three batteries approached from Michelsdorf, intending to set up camp for the night. As a report of a second French column reached Dolffs, he decided to attack quickly before it arrived. Signalling the attack by setting light to the windmill at Baudmannsdorf, he gave Maison enough warning to be able to form square and withdraw. However the French had not gone far when then were charged, their squares broken and their artillery captured. Maison was pursued to Hainau before the appearance of Puthod's Division forced Dolffs to break off his attack. The Prussians returned with 500 prisoners and five guns, the remaining guns having been left behind as their limbers had fled. The French lost 1,363 men, the Prussians 236 including Dolffs, who was mortally wounded. The action at Hainau did little to alter the overall picture but it greatly boosted Allied morale and sent a clear signal of their determination to continue the struggle.

The Allies fell back into Silesia, maintaining contact with the Austrian border and hoping for assistance. The Austrians started to mediate a cease-fire, a 36-hour pause in hostilities coming into force on 1 June. A formal cease-fire was then agreed, extending the temporary 36-hour pause. Both sides now spent the summer of 1813 frantically raising, training and equipping new formations for the forthcoming campaign. Behind the scenes desperate political manoeuvring continued as the Allies sought to woo the Austrians to their cause. The fighting was to continue in August and Austria finally threw her might behind the Allied coalition, tipping the scales decisively against Napoleon. The outcome was now almost inevitable and although the struggle continued into October, Napoleon's forces in Germany were finally crushed at Leipzig by the combined might of the Allied army. Leipzig sounded the death knell of Napoleon's Empire and the tide of war would now sweep across France itself. It was at Lützen and Bautzen that the tide had turned however.

THE BATTLEFIELDS TODAY

The Scharnhorst Memorial at Grossgörschen. Ceremonies take place here most years. (Photo courtesy of Ed Wimble of Clash-of-Arms)

Not far from Leipzig, the Lützen battlefield has remained largely unchanged since those dramatic events, although the southern edge of the battlefield, particularly the Allied starting point, has been subjected to strip-mining, so much so that the hill that hid the Russians and Prussians from Ney no longer exists. The village museum of Grossgörschen contains a diorama of the battle. Nearby is a memorial to the Prussian Scharnhorst, who was mortally wounded at the battle, as well as one to the battle itself, while in Starsiedel, 3 km west of Grossgörschen, there is a Prussian memorial at the entrance to the village. In Rahna is the grave of Christian Gottlieb Berger, a Prussian volunteer who died in the battle. The house in Kaja where Ney stayed on 2 May 1813 is marked with a plaque. It is at the entrance to the village on the road from Lützen. On the road from Grossgörschen to Pegau, 1 km south of Grossgörschen, near the site of the Monarch's Hill, is a memorial to Frederick William III. In Kleingörschen is a memorial to 2nd Lieutenant Franz Wilhelm Liebknecht, a Hessian who fought with the Württembergers on Napoleon's side at the battle. He died in combat against a Russian unit.

There are also several memorials on the Bautzen battlefield. A memorial to the dead of the battle can be found in the public cemetery in Bautzen itself. A Prussian memorial can be found on the summit of a line of hillocks 5 km to the north-east of Bautzen near the main road from Doberschütz to Kreckwitz.

BIBLIOGRAPHY

Brett-James, A., *Europe Against Napoleon*, London, 1970.

Chandler, D. *Campaigns of Napoleon*, London 1966.

Chandler, D. *Dictionary of the Napoleonic Wars*, London 1979.

Chandler, D. (ed.) *Napoleon's Marshals*, London 1987.

Esposito, V. and Elting, J. *A Military History and Atlas of the Napoleonic Wars*, reprinted London 1999.

Nafziger, G. *Lutzen & Bautzen – Napoleon's Spring Campaign of 1813*, Chicago 1992.

Petre, F.L., *Napoleon's Last Campaign in Germany – 1813*, London, 1912

Sherwig, J.M., *Guineas & Gunpowder – British Foreign Aid in the Wars with France, 1793-1815*,
    Cambridge MA, 1969

INDEX